"A classic piece of Catholic literature is *The Lives of the Saints*. What the Catholic Worker community has assembled here is an equal testament to the saintly lives of those who have crossed its threshold and brought Heaven a little closer to this broken world."

—**Martin Sheen**, actor and activist

"The beautifully written, often inspiring, and always fascinating obituaries in this volume are not about death, but about life, specifically, the lives of the men and women—holy, not so holy, and trying to be holy—who passed through the doors of the Catholic Worker Houses of Hospitality. Why not come to know some of the saints who are already praying for you from their posts in heaven?"

—**James Martin**, SJ, author of *My Life with the Saints*

"Open these pages to discover, or reconnect with, the meaning of life. It is not what we accomplish or amass. It is not our great works. It is who loves us, who grieves our deaths, who keeps saying our names. The people memorialized in this book built no fortunes but they lived, they mattered, they are remembered. This gentle reminder comes at the right time; amid the casual brutality and callous disregard that marks this epoch, we are invited to a new level of tenderness and awareness to the people around us."

—**Frida Berrigan**, author of *It Runs in the Family*

"A most unusual and beautiful book! Those remembered are a gallery of diverse characters touched with pathos and illness, humor and creativity, sin and grace. The writing lifts each one up with rich concreteness. Their lives give new meaning to the dignity of being a human person, a child of God, in every kind of circumstance. Read it and be inspired."

—**Elizabeth A. Johnson**, CSJ, Fordham University

"*Ambassadors of God* is the story of the heart of the Catholic Worker. This beautifully curated collection of obituaries gives us what no historical or theological study can do—it brings to life a community of souls who have lived complicated and wounded lives, often battling alcoholism or mental illness or both, yet who are also full of a generous, strong, and luminous humanity, valuable beyond reckoning."

—**Kate Hennessy**, author of *Dorothy Day: The World Will Be Saved By Beauty*

Ambassadors of God

Ambassadors of God

Selected Obituaries from *The Catholic Worker*

EDITED AND WITH AN
INTRODUCTION BY
Amanda W. Daloisio,
Dan Mauk, and
Terry Rogers

FOREWORD BY
Robert Ellsberg

RESOURCE *Publications* · Eugene, Oregon

AMBASSADORS OF GOD
Selected Obituaries from *The Catholic Worker*

Resource Publications
An Imprint of Wipf and Stock Publishers
199 W. 8th Ave., Suite 3
Eugene, OR 97401

www.wipfandstock.com

PAPERBACK ISBN: 978-1-4982-3950-9
HARDCOVER ISBN: 978-1-4982-3952-3
EBOOK ISBN: 978-1-4982-3951-6

Manufactured in the U.S.A.

Written material from *The Catholic Worker* used by permission.

Clarice Adams by Sarah Brook. Used by permission of the artist.

New York City Street Scene by Rita Corbin. Used by permssion of the artist.

Maryhouse, 55 East 3rd Street (1973–present) by Gary Donatelli. Used by permission of the artist.

St. Joseph House, 36 East 1st Street (1968–present) by Gary Donatelli. Used by permission of the artist.

Peter Maurin Farm, Staten Island (1950–1964) by James Forest. Used by permission of the artist.

St. Joseph House, 175 Chrystie Street (1961–1968) by James Forest. Used by permission of the artist.

Preston Lewis by Tony Gawron. Used by permission of *The Catholic Worker*.

Smokey Joe by Tony Gawron. Used by permission of *The Catholic Worker*.

The Kitchen at St. Joseph House, 36 East 1st Street (1968–present) by Louise Giovannoni. Used by permission of *The Catholic Worker*.

Johanna by M. Eileen Lawter. Used by permission of the artist.

Josephine by Ann Leggett. Used by permission of the Estate of Ann Leggett.

St. Lawrence was a deacon and martyr of the early Roman church. His work was to collect offerings from the church members and to distribute them as alms to the poor. One day the Roman officials ordered him to hand over the treasures of the church—all its gold and silver—to the authorities. Instead, he brought with him a crowd of poor people on whom the church's resources had been spent.

"Here," he said. "Here are the treasures of the church."

Modern society calls the beggar
bum and panhandler
and gives him the bum's rush.
But the Greeks used to say
that people in need
are the ambassadors of the gods.

PETER MAURIN

Contents

CONTENTS

Foreword

BY ROBERT ELLSBERG

AMONG THE READINGS FOR the Feast of All Saints is this text from Ecclesiasticus:

> Let us now praise famous men, and our fathers that begat us.
>
> The Lord hath wrought great glory by them through his great power from the beginning . . . .
>
> And some there be, which have no memorial; who are perished, as though they had never been; and are become as though they had never been born. (44:1, 2, 9)

That text supplied the title for James Agee's Depression-era classic, *Let Us Now Praise Famous Men*. It is an ironic title, since Agee's book describes some of the poorest and least consequential people of his time—white sharecroppers in Alabama. But those who read Agee's book with care could see that it was not simply a sociological exposé, but, as he put it, "an independent inquiry into certain normal predicaments of human divinity." These poor folk were among those of whom the author of Ecclesiasticus sings, who leave no great mark in history, who have "perished as though they had never been born," and yet whose righteous deeds live on, if only in the memory of God.

The men and women memorialized in this extraordinary volume, *Ambassadors of God*, certainly left no great mark in history. Nor are they remembered here for their righteous deeds, but because for some time, whether brief or over many years, they occupied a place in that particular ecological niche in New York City known as the Catholic Worker. There they were noticed and seen; there they contributed their peculiarities, gifts, transgressions, and moments of transcendence to the rich soup of

ix

community life; there they were recognized as more than the sum of their poor parts—as children of God.

To suggest that these men and women are examples of ordinary sanctity is not to sugarcoat their evident faults and failings. What is remarkable about these memorials is the lack of sentimentality. We learn of their subjects' colorful eccentricities, their capacity for celebration, their sometimes startling insights and prophetic observations. But we are not spared their anger, their prejudices, the wounds they were capable of inflicting on themselves or on those around them. At the Catholic Worker they found they did not have to earn their place in the family. They were accepted, they were welcomed, they found a home.

Unlike typical obituaries, these stories are often marked by a certain mystery. Where did these characters come from? What kind of work or life preceded their arrival at the Catholic Worker? Were they loved? Did they travel? Did they leave any noticeable accomplishments? We see them as they appeared at the end of their lives. For all the diversity that may have marked their origins, they shared in common a final destination.

But that destination was evidently more than a pauper's grave. It is called the communion of saints. Whatever past was lost to memory, they did not disappear as if they had never been born. Among those who knew them, broke bread with them, and loved them for a time—and now also among the readers of this book—their memory lives on.

Introduction

"THE BITTER COLD, COMBINED with lack of food, caused the death of an unidentified man who sought refuge on the pier at 127th St. and the Hudson River."

These words begin a brief notice in the January 1936 issue of *The Catholic Worker*. Deep in the Great Depression such deaths were common, and publishing the scanty news of this man's death was a way for *The Catholic Worker* to do what an obituary is supposed to do—to honor the unique reality of someone's life and death. This man's death was his own, but for readers of the newspaper he represented all those who die poor and alone, hungry and cold.

The Catholic Worker has published many obituaries since that first notice. Most of them commemorate the lives of people who lived in poverty, sometimes in severe destitution, in or near the New York Catholic Worker communities, both urban and rural. They were written by people who knew the deceased personally, and in many cases shared daily life with them. The purpose of this book is to focus on such remembrances because of their special character as tributes to those otherwise forgotten.

The Catholic Worker has included obituaries such as these over the years to honor the courage with which their subjects have faced lives of physical and mental suffering. You will find social history in this collection, as well as a theological perspective that is essential to the Catholic Worker: the presence of Christ in those disregarded by the world. These stories have been told year after year to remind us that those who are poor and destitute among us are often the ones to teach us holiness, and that God delights to welcome them into the communion of saints.

These stories and many others have been part of the Catholic Worker movement since it began in New York City in 1933. Welcoming the poor and the stranger is one of the most important responsibilities of a Catholic

1

Worker community. The movement's way of life is rooted in the Gospel as understood by our founders, Dorothy Day and Peter Maurin: voluntary poverty, opposition to killing and structural violence, and the daily carrying out of the Works of Mercy—offering food, clothing, shelter, and companionship to those in need.

In her book *Waiting on God*, the philosopher Simone Weil writes: "The capacity to give one's attention to a sufferer is a very rare and difficult thing; it is almost a miracle; it is a miracle." What we read in these pages is attention at its most prayerful, and it concerns the very particulars of daily life. Many of those we read about were mentally ill, suffered from addiction, or were severely disabled. They were also honest and brave, funny, creative, and often incredibly generous. They lead us to shift our focus from those who are in our lives through family or by choice, and to fix our hearts on those whom we might not otherwise choose to know.

This book is an historical offering, a sampling of those who have come before us to live and work at the New York Catholic Worker. It is also a spiritual offering. Stay awake, it says, and pay attention to the details of life and to one another. In a time when human worth is measured by what we produce or what we accumulate, this book offers a reflection on another way.

It is a blessing for us who never knew the lives profiled in this book to have a chance to know them, and to be grateful to those who paid such close attention. What kind of miracles could be expected if all of us could pay this kind of attention to the poor around us?

The Editors

Cold and Hunger Is Fatal to Man on 127th St. Pier

The Catholic Worker January 1936

THE BITTER COLD, COMBINED with lack of food, last week caused the death of an unidentified man who sought refuge on the pier at 127th Street and the Harlem River.

In the inside pocket of a threadbare black overcoat were found several crusts of bread, a prayer book, and rosary beads. A label bore "M. Barry, 650 W. 173rd St." Detectives could find no one there who knew the man. The body was removed to Bellevue Morgue.

Mr. Breen

The Catholic Worker June 1939

[This article and the two that follow were unsigned. The likely author is Dorothy Day, who was the editor of the newspaper during those years.—The Editors]

SURELY EVERYONE WHO CAME to see us at the Catholic Worker must have met Mr. Breen. He was an unforgettable figure, over six feet tall, with a mane of iron grey hair, sometimes wearing a beard so that he looked like Chief Justice Hughes, and at other times clean shaven. His leg had been broken and not mended properly so that he had to walk slowly with a cane and this only added to his dignity. His progress was slow and stately rather than halting.

He came to us six years ago when we were living on Fifteenth Street, sent to us by George Shuster of *The Commonweal*, for whom he had done many book reviews. His career as a newspaper man was long and varied—he had been Sunday editor of the *Washington Post*, he had been one of the editors on the old *World*—it is even rumored that he had been Mr. Coolidge's press agent. He was born in Ireland and educated at Clongowes Wood. There was never a man in public life that he had not met and about whom he had not some story to tell.

Misfortune had fallen upon him and he took it with dignity. For a time he had stayed at the Municipal Lodging House. Though I believe an attempt had been made to keep him on relief, he had had a fight with the relief visitor—he was a haughty soul, and it was probably about some world event rather than about his own situation. He was always on the verge of using his cane on someone who differed from him in his views of Father Coughlin, the CIO, collective security, or the interracial problem.

He enjoyed his stay in the Municipal Lodging House and had many tales to tell about his adventures there. He used to threaten every week or so to go back there just to hear me forbid him.

He used to spend the day with us on Fifteenth Street and return at night to the room provided him a few blocks away. Later when we moved to Charles Street, he entered the house of hospitality and for the last four and a half years has lived with us. He always had a great desire to work and for awhile went through the day labor exchanges conscientiously. Then for a number of years he acknowledged subscriptions and notes that came in and he probably covered thousands of our little pictured cards with his fine graceful script and slightly old-fashioned sentiments. Occasionally, however, in a state of ire, he would express himself most frankly and forceably and get us into a jam. One time a friend in California suggested that he start some work along our lines and Mr. Breen answered him haughtily. Never could the work be done as well as the New York group did it, he thought. Our correspondent in high wrath wrote back and wanted to know who we thought we were, specially enlightened by the Holy Ghost, sitting on the right hand of God, or what? It took a five-page letter to pacify him.

It was Mr. Breen's custom to sit in the window in the front office on Charles Street and greet visitors as they came in. He also loved fresh air, and in winter it was hard to persuade him to keep the window closed by his side. It was his special delight to answer the telephone when the rest of the crowd were out to Mass in the morning and on one occasion we arrived back in the office to hear him responding forceably "Hell, yes!" as he banged down the receiver. On being asked to whom he was replying, he growled, "She wanted to know if we approved of the violence in the building strike!"

It was probably because of Mr. Breen that we started our spiritual reading at table. It effectively put an end to controversy. He never complained once of food served, and some of the meals were abominable. We used to accuse Charlie of burning everything he cooked. (We were living on oatmeal and spaghetti that summer and scorching never improved them, but Mr. Breen never complained.) But he would start an argument about John L. Lewis, for instance. And when Mr. Breen argued, he roared. He was like an old lion.

Down here on Mott Street he came finally to love our neighbors although he distrusted them all as foreigners first. He liked to go down and sit in the kitchen where coffee was being prepared for the bread line, or out in the circulation office by the door to watch the activities on the street.

Even these last months when he was so ill, he tried to get down the stairs to participate in the life of the community and it was hard to keep him quiet in bed.

His was a good death. He had been ill many times this past year and three times he had to go to Columbus Hospital for some weeks. They treated him with great respect and consideration there and he loved the little Mother who used to come in to see him. But he did not want to die in the hospital, he always said, and we always assured him that he would die at home with us.

The night before his last day he had a fearful time breathing. His heart was very bad, and he struggled mightily for air. The doctor from next door was in to see him every few hours and she eased him as much as she could by injections. At one in the morning I called Father Kett of St. Andrew's, who had long been an old friend of Mr. Breen's and used to visit him often. He made his confession and was anointed, and as we said the prayers for the dying by his bedside, he made the responses too. His mind was perfectly clear, and after the priest had left, he lay there praying aloud. "God has been very good to me," he said again and again. "I am very happy."

We sat up with him all that night and during the next day there were always two or three in the room with him. He was not conscious that day. All through the long afternoon we sat there with him. Outside the children were playing in the yard, calling out joyously to each other. On the rear of the front house the sun shone and the shadows of pigeons flecked the walls as they wheeled in the sun. Downstairs supper was being prepared for the forty-five other members of the household, and every now and then someone would come up to stay awhile and pray.

At five-thirty, just after the dinner bell rang, he died, quietly and peacefully. He looked very noble and kingly, stretched out there in death.

I was glad for him, because he had suffered much. He had prayed for death daily because he could not work anymore. He must have written ten thousand careful little post cards. He had always tried to help in every way he could. He had handed over to us with pride and joy the money he received from book reviews, and some of that money had gone to buy a pig for Tamar on the farm and stockings and galoshes for me. He had true dignity in that he had never rebelled at his poverty, in that he had risen above his surroundings always.

He died leaving nothing, possessing nothing. If he had anything extra he always passed it on to others. But of course there was his cane, that cane he used to shake at people in arguments. Many a time he had threatened to wrap it around the neck of one or another around the house. That cane now is mine. And when I use it on the hills around the farm, I shall think of Mr. Breen, part of our family, who is now gone. He is happy now, as he was happy before his death; and we too are glad that he is released from his long agony and is having rest from his labors. May he rest in peace.

Peter Maurin Farm, Staten Island (1950–1964)
Artist: James Forest

Stephen Hergenhan

The Catholic Worker March 1942

IF YOU GO DOWN to the Brooklyn Bridge, take a Madison Street bus, get off at Jackson Street and walk to the river, you find there St. Rose's Home for Incurable Cancer. You go through Greek, Italian, Spanish, and Jewish neighborhoods. It's just a good walk from the Catholic Worker office and for weeks now someone has been getting down every day to see Steve Hergenhan, dear friend and fellow worker, who was transferred there from Roosevelt Hospital last month.

Three weeks ago he was baptized, received the Sacrament of Penance, was anointed. Three sacraments in one afternoon. He lay there, smelling a gardenia which I had brought in to him, a little sample of the sweetness of heaven.

"I wanted to gather my loose ends together," he said, when he accepted the ministrations of the priest. "I've been working with the Catholic Worker for the past nine years, ever since it started, and I am a Catholic."

He was cheerful and calm. He lay there with eyes closed and smiled. "There has been much harshness and some gentlenesses in my life," he said, "and now there is more of the gentlenesses." But some days he is not so happy.

"Here I am, a helpless old fool, dying," he said this afternoon. "Can't do a thing for myself, can't use my feet or hands, and scarcely my head."

Outside the birds were perched on the statue of St. Joseph in the little garden by the side of the window. Steve has a private room (only one other patient) and there are two large dormitories facing the river. Only once has he been able to get out to the sun parlor since he came to the hospital. Now he doesn't leave his bed.

"But I can do nothing," he states. I think of all the things he has done around the Catholic Worker, all the labor he has put in, all the speeches he has made at our Wednesday night meetings.

He came to us, a friend of Peter Maurin, when our office was on Fifteenth Street. He helped keep the meeting going there. He and Peter used to have dialogues, discussing Nazism, Communism, Fascism, and Catholicism. Steve was always a communitarian personalist, he said, but once he had tried living alone.

Before Peter had known him he had built a house for himself (he was a real craftsman) up near Suffern. The taxes were raised so constantly to pay for the automobile roads that he both couldn't and wouldn't pay them. So he lost his house, built alone by himself, and ended up in the Municipal Lodging House in New York. He used to spend his day in the libraries, in the parks, engaged in discussion. He wrote some articles on the "Muni" which we published, and which brought forth visits from city officials who drove up in a big car, and asked us plaintively why we had not taken the matter up with them before publishing the articles. Steve himself had, and had been threatened with the Psychopathic in consequence.

He did not want to sell his labor, so after he came to live with us he used to give his services to others. He started gardens at Staten Island; he wrote articles for the farm page. Also he built entirely a five-room house down on our farm.

A friend had given us a thousand dollars to make payment, in return for which we were supposed to deed her a corner and build her a house. So now she has three acres and a house, built of brick and lumber and field stone, with two cisterns, a good cellar, an attic, and a beautiful fireplace in the living room. There were also built-in benches, desk, and bookcases. A lovely job. The Nova Scotia cooperative housing estimate of labor costs of such a house was nine hundred dollars.

"And here I lie helpless," Peter's old friend says. So I started chiding him, and his attitude toward work, and he who loved work and who always had been such a worker, listened in pleased surprise. I was giving him some of the ideas that Father Hugo had given us at our retreat this summer.

"There are three kinds of work, physical, and that is hard and demands self-discipline; mental, and that is harder; and last of all spiritual, and that is hardest—the kind of work everyone is trying to get out of all the time.

"Here you have been a worker all your life, you loved to work, you had a philosophy of labor. You like physical work and mental work, too. You liked to read, and you liked to argue, and you spent hours and hours at it. And now you can't read and you can't work and you've got to begin exercising some of your spiritual faculties. You've got to begin exercising Faith, Hope, and Charity. They are very weak. You haven't got much faith in men, nor much hope for them, though you've always been more charitable than you'd like anyone to believe, in your 'harshnesses.' You've washed clothes for people, and fed people and worked for people you have not particularly liked, nor admired, nor would have chosen for your associates. But you need to exercise those virtues, so that they become strong. If you don't exercise your physical muscles they get weak, so you have to exercise these spiritual ones, and that is the work God wants you to do now. That's probably why he laid you so low.

"But you still have to move mountains. And you can do it, even if you don't do it with pick and shovel. It would be lots easier to use the pick and shovel, but you've got to use the only effective means, Prayer."

I talked at length like this because he was always asking for serious talk. When I came in he'd tell me to sit down and talk. "I can't talk, I can't read. But you and Julia give me ideas and so I can think."

Today he was groaning a bit over his helplessness as I came in. "But Sister Stanislaus says that you have a fine spirit," I told him.

"That means my spirit is broken," he said sadly. But he knew it was not. We began at once talking about the spiritual combat, the sword of the spirit. He had fought all his life, and now he had been stripped of every weapon but the spiritual. God must have thought he was strong enough, otherwise he would not have handed this affliction to him. God was feeding him the strong meat of suffering, not milk for babes. He was giving him some last jobs to do.

"To move mountains," he was murmuring, as I left this afternoon. And he looked pleasantly determined, as though he had set himself to the job.

The world is engaged in a life-and-death struggle of mind and brawn. On all fronts it is suffering defeats, and the blows from every side come thick and fast. But Steve Hergenhan, fellow worker in Christ, lies on a bed in St. Rose's Cancer Hospital and sets himself to moving mountains.

P.S.: The day before we went to press, Steve died in his sleep, after just a few months of illness. We ask our readers to pray for him.

Big Dan Is Dead

The Catholic Worker December 1944

HE DIED ON THE Feast of the Immaculate Conception, the twelfth anniversary of the starting of *The Catholic Worker*. He was our oldest apostle in point of service. Everybody knew him as Big Dan and visitors to New York from all over the country often were introduced to *The Catholic Worker* by seeing him selling the paper in front of Macy's or on Fourteenth Street. These last years he had been working as a taxi driver, but he kept up his interest in the work, he carried bundles to the post office, brought us food for the breadline, and came faithfully to the office every few weeks to see if there was anything he could do to help.

He was a huge person, tall and stout, and it was hard to get clothes to fit. He used to fill the doorway as he came in shouting always—"Everybody happy?" and everybody in the office would groan "NO!" His second words usually were, "Anything to eat?" but he more often brought food than ate it with us these last years.

Big Dan came to us back in 1933, during the depth of the Depression, when *The Catholic Worker* was housed on Fifteenth Street. He had been looking for work and tramping the streets of the city, and he told us frankly that his feet hurt. Margaret, our Lithuanian fellow worker who was doing the cooking at that time, hospitably offered to let him soak his feet; and that was his introduction to us all, a large genial man, with a round happy face and sparkling eyes, sitting there in the kitchen soaking his tired feet. He stayed for supper that night, and Peter engaged him in conversation about jobs and manual labor, the dignity of poverty and work. He always listened to Peter with great respect and lowered his great voice in talking to him. He could not resist interspersing what Peter termed wise crackings, however, and Peter, with his French mind, would pucker up his face and try to understand what was the point that Big Dan was trying to make.

After that first visit, Dan felt entirely at home and took over the sale of the paper on the streets. It did one's heart and soul good to see him standing on the corner of Fourteenth Street and Broadway with a bundle of papers, shouting—in opposition to someone who was shouting "Read *The Daily Worker!*"—"Read *The Catholic Worker* daily!" Often when he saw me, either on Fourteenth, Thirty-fourth, or Forty-second Street, mischief overcame him and he added to his shouting, "Read *The Catholic Worker*— Romance on every page!" and on one occasion, "Read *The Catholic Worker*, and here comes the editor walking down the street!"

He had an immediate appreciation of the personalist technique of the movement. He made friends with all those who were carrying sandwich signs advertising the gypsy tea room, or a children's furniture store, or garments on the installment plan, and found out their needs and tried to supply them from our clothes room or food stocks. Margaret, the cook, used to chase him with the rolling pin when he raided the ice box or pantry. He used to mimic her and dodge out of the room, begging her not to "tell the *pasture* on him." (Margaret always called the pastor the *pasture*, much to Dan's delight. He had a collection of her sayings with which he is probably regaling the angels in heaven now.)

He sold the paper, he helped us move families who were evicted, he helped to take care of old Mr. Breen whose room he shared, he walked with us on picket lines during the picketing of Ohrbach's, the National Biscuit Company, the Mexican consulate, the German consulate.

He was a city boy, born in Jersey City and knowing only New York and his own home town. But he helped us look for the farm which we later obtained at Easton. Mrs. Porter Chandler, a reader and benefactor of the paper, loaned us her car during the icy winter to look for a place, and Big Dan did the driving. When we finally found the hilltop farm at Easton, he climbed with us to the very top of the hill and then lay down in the center of the alfalfa field and looked up at the blue April sky. "This is the place," he told us happily, and proceeded to take a nap while we discussed acreage and payments with the owner.

Always on these trips he reminded us of the Angelus, and at the stroke of twelve or six we would pray as we sped through the countryside. And it was at the stroke of the Angelus that he died, on the Feast of the Immaculate Conception, in the House of Calvary, surrounded by his family and the friends for whom he had worked these past years, before the gas shortage made him take up taxi driving. They were our friends, too, since it was through the generosity of Miss Gertrude Burke and the House of Calvary that we have the use of the house of hospitality on Mott Street.

Dan Orr was one of those "called to be saints" of the Catholic Worker. He was always serving others, always happy, always generous. One never heard him say an unkind word—there was never malice or detraction in his speech. He was one of the "little ones," good and pure of heart, faithful and kind. We are happy to have known him and to have worked with him.

He was buried with a Solemn High Mass from St. Lucy's Church in Jersey City, and may God rest his generous soul. Big Dan, please pray for all of us you have left behind.

Josephine

Artist: Ann Leggett

Josephine

BY JEAN FOREST

The Catholic Worker June 1964

THE FIRST TIME I came across Josephine at the Catholic Worker was during one of her appearances at a Friday Night Meeting. She was wearing a low-cut yellow evening dress which she told us she wore especially for weekends. I couldn't believe my eyes—she looked like a grotesque, aged Ophelia or a caricature of a fairy queen. She was eventually shuffled from the meeting after causing some disturbance. Our next encounter was in the clothing room where I distributed clothes. Each week she would appear with a different and imaginative tale of what happened to the clothes we had given her the last week. Very often, it was the tale of some interesting thief she had entrusted with them. It didn't matter, for I never could refuse her. I found, quite to my amazement, that I really liked and enjoyed her stories.

One can get impersonal to the people one serves. It's the easiest way out on the nerves. Josephine never allowed anyone to treat her impersonally. With her it wasn't business or a handout; it was a person-to-person encounter. She worked on you until you had to respond positively or negatively. When she asked you for a bandage (she was usually bruised either from falls or beatings), you knew better than to procrastinate for a minute. Her needs were immediate and she'd tolerate no delay. Not that she was a nag. It was never that way because of her fantastic sense of humor. Fantastic, in the face of living on the streets (she preferred their freedom and excitement). She was an alcoholic with an ailing liver, always bruised and abused, begging for the next meal and drink. How did she escape despair? The answer may be in the mystery of her humor. When feeling especially exuberant she serenaded the kitchen and office with her most prized possession—a harmonica. The Bowery was a way of life which she accepted and, you might say, made the most of. She would tell a variety of stories of how she got here. She claimed to have become an alcoholic while a nurse. She said she had a husband somewhere and a child. She could have been any age from fifty to eighty.

Her last years were spent as a music maker and clown—harming no one and bringing laughter to some. She died in the hospital ward of the poor. It was a hard life which she managed to transcend—as though by magic.

Mike Herniak

by Bob Gilliam

The Catholic Worker February 1970

MIKE HERNIAK, OUR "RUSSIAN" Mike, is dead. We loved him. I would like to make him real for you, but I am not sure how. The written word is pale. If we could sit across a table, I would try to tell his wonderful stories. They must be heard. It would be a gift, a grace, a joy. But I mustn't be romantic. He was also impossible. He drank far too much and stayed drunk for months. He was less than clean when he was drinking. He was demanding and he could raise more hell than anyone we know.

Mike died in his mid-fifties and he looked seventy. Everything was wrong with him—heart, liver, lungs, stomach. He was tall, about six feet, and thin. He was stoop-shouldered and limped slightly. He had a small face on the end of a long neck. His face was thin except for the odd pouches in his cheeks. His eyes were lively and deep set under full eyebrows. When he was sober he seemed to be watching everything. There played constantly across his face a small, sly, knowing smile.

My words limp. Let Mike speak for himself. These are the things he told me. Things I will never forget.

Mike made life hard for us. Harder, but better. I remember once he asked me for a second package of tobacco only hours after I had given him the first one. I chided him, told him I couldn't give it to him, told him tobacco was not so cheap. He said, in his way, halting, gesticulating, composing, "What can I do, Bobby, my brothers are in need. They say, Mike, can I have a paper? Mike, have you got tobacco? Mike, roll me one? I cannot refuse, Bobby, my brothers are in need. Remember, Bobby, whatever you do unto these the least of my brothers. Yeah." I gave him the tobacco.

Another time I was telling Mike he ought to think about doing a little work on the paper. He reminded me, "I built those tables, Bobby. They're good tables, but I can't do like I used to. But there's different kinds of work—physical work, spiritual work. I been doin' spiritual work, Bobby. Teachin', prayin', helpin', guidin'." He was.

This summer Mike was in Bellevue Hospital and we visited often. He was there during the moon shot and the self-congratulating hysteria which followed it. "Bobby, those people must know a lot, but they don't seem to know what's important. If a man has a family and his son, brother, nephew has no place to stay, nothing to put on, and not enough to eat, does the man buy a new boat or a second car or does he take care of the family? Yeah. Well, he oughta take care of the family. By my way of thinkin', we're just all one big family and, Bobby, there's lots of people with no place to stay, nothing to put on, and not enough to eat. They oughta take care of the family first and then go to the moon. Yeah. They seem to know a lot but they don't seem to know what's important." These are the wisest words I remember hearing at that time.

I remember the day I found out about Mike's death. I walked, crying a little, and thought about him. Mike had suffered terribly. He had been on the skids for more than twenty years—in and out of hospitals and jails, working at crummy jobs, living in flop houses, drinking and panhandling, sleeping in doorways. He lived for awhile with our friend Ed Brown. Brown says Mike was the kindest, most deeply Christian person he had ever lived with. I feel somehow that if we can begin to see Mike, to listen to his life, we will be a long way toward understanding the mystery of the Catholic Worker—and much more. In the eyes of the world he was a bum, less than nothing. In fact, he was gigantically real. He was fully alive, and despite the horror of his life, more than intact. He embraced his life like a vocation. He had a rich and varied internal life—he thought, he felt, he prayed. Every man is precious. Every man is an end and not a means. Every man is to be treated like Christ. We mouth these hard, hard words but every now and then we meet a man, a man on the absolute bottom, a man who, the world says, doesn't exist; and he shows us, so that we cannot escape it, the truth of those words. In knowing Mike we were touched and burned with the hard, deep, living truth of those words.

I remember a talk Mike and I had this summer at Bellevue. "You know, I been thinkin' about the old saying 'you can't take it with you.' Yeah. Well, I believe that's true. Fame, fortune, recognition, medals. They are as nothing. The only thing you can take with you is what you did, what you said, what you are. The only thing that is essential and primary is when you stand before the seat and the Lord says, 'When I was hungry, did you feed me?' Can you answer yes? 'When I was naked, did you clothe me?' Can you answer yes? 'When I was homeless, did you shelter me?' Can you answer yes? Yeah. And how does the rest of it go, Bobby?" And I finished the passage from Matthew about the beloved of the Father entering into that sweet place that is prepared for them.

Mike said, "That's right, Bobby. I wish that to be said to you. I could not ask for more. May you have eternal life."

We wish that to be said to you, dear Mike, dear brother and teacher. Rest in Peace.

Smokey Joe
Artist: Tony Gawron

More about Smokey (1903–1970)

BY PATRICK JORDAN

The Catholic Worker December 1970

SMOKEY JOE HAS LEFT us, and indeed there is not a little sorrow. After completing almost sixty-seven years of rugged contention, on September 29 he succumbed, at home, and at peace in his sudden end.

It was not as if there had been no warnings. In his last months they were written all over, visible as flags, in the swelling of his joints and the stony hardening of his brow. But he would not be touched, or moved to see a doctor, and he endured the weighsome breaking of his lungs and heart until the final battle was won.

Smokey was ever ready to take up the fray. He did so for peace or other dubious causes. He was, to his toes, NAVY, and I can once recall addressing him as "Sir," only to be corrected. He never was indeed an officer, he said, and must never be addressed as one. His was a courageous but never wholly disciplined impetuosity. He tackled stairways, charging them, even to the last. It was as if he was again heading to the pitcher's mound, the citadel of his early and only days of glory.

In those days, as a pitcher for the Navy, he had once defeated "Rockefeller's" College All Stars. ("Rockefeller" for Smokey meant anything that was rich and supposedly untouchable, and he never ceased showing his contempt for such overstuffed airs by bursting their balloon whenever given the chance.) The band had played after that victorious game, and he was ever after the hero. Only two other episodes ranked with this in his hall of memories, the winning of a spelling bee in seventh grade, and the serving of Mass, the latter which he always mentioned with a very wry sparkle that watched his listener's face fall into disbelief. This inevitably brought a chorus of his best, "I am a bad boy, I is, I is, I is!"

It was the impetuosity and a certain boisterousness that led Smokey to the Bowery. Eventually he arrived at Mott Street and the Catholic Worker. During those early Depression years he conducted the coffee line, and in one emergency it was his tough veins that gave blood by direct transfusion to a dying girl and saved her small life. No doubt this was a greater achievement than his pitching victory, but Smokey found it harder to take credit for doing good than for winning ball games.

Several times Smokey battled for his own life. Once he was raked by a fuel truck along the Bowery, and remained for months in a hospital. His arms, legs, and hips were badly fractured, and when he left the hospital he was never to walk or look the same. In fact, he resembled a man pasted together by a child, his limbs like those of a snarled tree.

His other critical battle resulted from a delicate eye operation. His cataracts were removed. Characteristically, he had told the doctor to proceed "full speed ahead," that he was willing to risk blindness if it would be for the betterment of mankind.

Smokey had a remarkable presence to the case at hand, a singleness of purpose. The latter led him to a Catholic Worker desk almost every day of his final ten years. He addressed the new subscriptions, and must have autographed more papers than almost anyone in the century. His script was distinctive, hurkey-jerkey, so individualistic as to be a signature. He was a Catholic Worker through and through. His faithfulness was a real achievement in the rolling gears of New York City.

His was also a very real simplicity. When he spoke of "Mommy Day," for example, and beamed at reading the paper and the appeal which he spent his final days working over, one knew there was no put-on. It was the same openness that remembered your name and face, perhaps even your address, over the long years. It was a care which brought him to pray every night and each morning for Peter Maurin and "all the great Catholic Workers" down the years.

On top of that, Smokey, this unusual sailor, was rich in poverty. Indeed, he was the poorest man here, and seemed to have an aversion for things which would only clutter his way. He died without even a pair of shorts, and with only the shirt he was to wear the next day. On opening his suitcase, only bits of dust and an ancient blue laundry tag remained. I recall that once when Smokey's eye had caught the flash of a new shirt, he set out a claim with untypical swiftness. Then, after a moment's thought, he returned this superfluity, saying he already had one and that this one should be given to someone who really needed it.

When the policeman who examined his belongings discovered several lone pennies in Smokey's pocket, he directed to have done with them what undoubtedly (and very importantly) Smokey would have done with them himself. "Put these in some poor box," remarked the officer.

The fullest aspect of Smokey's poverty was his gratitude. A good dinner never passed without his OK to the cooks, a personal recommendation of "I thank you, ladies." Occasionally he would sing one of his songs for them, or let his tattoos dance in the ripple of his muscles. And then he would be off for his brew, the crown and purpose of his day.

I think we'll always remember Smokey for his straightforwardness. He could terminate harebrained discussions with one swift and exacting invective. He hated to be preached at, especially about religion, and his judgments of character were usually precise and accurate. He could spot a "phony" around the corner. Furthermore, when pushed to it, he would let you and the world know his graphic feelings about it.

Such are the makings of the hidden treasure. When so many died this spring, Smokey, more than any other, took these things to himself. It was then he prepared himself for death, a death which up to then and to the rest of us seemed much farther and happily removed.

The night before he died, Smokey went to bed as if something had been resolved. He had been sitting on the stoop and had tried to cheer up a young fellow who sometimes came to our door. Then he had gone up the stairs unassisted. It was the last time we saw that unique walk, what Bob Gilliam once described as a sand crab walking sideways. A later inspection found Smokey resting peacefully. And then it was over.

Nothing more is needed except words of the psalm: "But I am a beggar and poor: the Lord is careful for me" (40:17). The Lord is very careful for you, indeed.

Catherine Tarangul, A Lament

BY STEVE NOWLING

The Catholic Worker January 1974

THEY TELL ME, CATHERINE, that you are dead, but how could they know? How could they know that if you could die, it would have been years ago when your five-year-old son was stricken with spinal meningitis, or when your husband abandoned wife and child, or when you walked Times Square each day selling trinkets and candy to pay for rent and food for you and your growing boy, or when fire destroyed your last apartment and took the life of your son?

No, Catherine, you did not die. You continued living and struggling year after year after year. By normal reckoning, maybe seventy-four years. But you are so much older, Catherine, for who can count all the minutes that were years as you sat in one cramped room after another with the bed sagging, the battered chest of drawers, the leaking sink, and the single, bare fluorescent bulb hanging in the center, with the long string switch trailing almost to the bed? How many hundreds of years did you sit staring out that dirty window with the drooping venetian blinds at the other women's sons, and wonder why yours was never allowed to run and laugh and sing and go to school and fall in love and bring you grandbabies to hold?

They tell me, Catherine, that you have died, but that is not possible. Your demand for justice has not yet been fulfilled. "My rights! My rights and the rights of my son! Tell me, Stevie, who is America? Is America Rockefeller? No! America is the people. And Jesus is for all the people, too. Right? That is why Rockefeller and the others killed him. Oi, oi. Where is the justice? I want the justice. I read the Bible once. It is good to read it once. But after that, what good is it? Listen to me, Stevie, and I will make a man of you. We must see with our hearts, but then we must speak with our mouths. Then we will have justice. See!"

Yes, Catherine, I think I see. But you know, Catherine, I have been told that you are dead. I know it is not so, for where is the justice?

CATHERINE TARANGUL
24 November 1973—RIP

St. Joseph House, 175 Chrystie Street (1961–1968)

Artist: James Forest

John McMullan

BY PATRICK JORDAN

The Catholic Worker January 1974

"MY ASPENS DEAR, . . . ALL felled, felled, are all felled." Thus the brute opening of Hopkins' stunning poem "Binsey Poplars—felled 1879." So we record the death of another of our family's fairest trees, John McMullan, felled by a crashing fall in Christmastide 1973.

He was born in Northern Ireland in 1908. His family was Catholic, but owned a small farm in Kilrea near Derry. John was baptized in the local Church of St. Mary, and as a young man worked the family farm with his father and three brothers. In the early 30s he immigrated to America, following by several months his younger sister Mary, who had come to live with an uncle in Brooklyn. John paid the uncle rent, and was soon taken on by a fellow Irishman, digging ditches for the gas company. He implied it was downright fortuitous to have a job in those years. Other jobs were to follow before the war as a maintenance worker and as a short-order cook in Sheepshead Bay.

When the war broke out, John served in the U.S. Coast Guard. He spoke about his days in Norfolk the way a high-seas sailor speaks of ports across the Pacific. In this there was the trim pride which was a pervasive aspect of his manner.

After the war John returned to live with his sister, who was then settled in a small town near the Jersey shore. But for John the place lacked the fluidity of the city, the excitement and anonymity. He soon moved back to New York.

John was an urban man despite his origins. On several occasions he visited the Catholic Worker farm at Tivoli, only to return quickly to the city. The slowness of the farm was more oppressive to him than the chaos of the First Street house. Here he met scores of visitors and volunteers, kept up with the daily newspapers, and could talk with numerous friends. Here, too, he had easy access to the "punch" that was his weakness, and the surety of a place where he was needed.

John first came to the Worker at 175 Chrystie Street. He lived on the Bowery then, at the Palace Hotel (one of those euphemisms for the circles of hell). Serving the soup at St. Joseph House alongside Wong, he came to be known as "Irish John." Together with Mary Galligan, Wong and John set a gruff but welcoming tone that was the style of the soup line for years. The soup, made and served from the ranks, was appetizing to the men.

Eventually John followed Charlie Keefe and Jack Cook as proprietor of the soup itself. He took great pride in this, arising at 4:30 in the morning and walking the dark blocks from the hotel to the First Street house. Several times he was mugged at this early hour, but eventually the abductors came to realize it was "John the soup cook," and allowed him to pass unassaulted.

John loved the quiet hours of the day, the early hours when he was alone with the freshly made coffee and the just-boiling beans. He called these "the best hours." He would set the table for breakfast and cook the oatmeal. Then would come daylight, Arthur with the paper, and finally the bustle, the onslaught. He would begin looking toward the night's television and the next morning.

I can't say I always ate John's soup or liked it. Sometimes it was superb, but other times it was a stomach-boggling concoction. But for all that, it sustained hundreds of us for years. When asked what kind of soup he had made today, John would answer "soup de jour" (in the manner he had learned from Charlie Keefe), or "oriental soup today." He would say it in a gleeful style. Then throwing back his head, he'd laugh till his face and forehead turned red.

John had, as I mentioned, a sense of the line. Seldom did he lord it over our guests, although the temptation was there. Instead he had greetings for many a man, greetings that were personal and bespoke comradeship. He would lend money to some, give cigarettes to others. When Mary died and Wong went upstairs to work on the paper, John felt somehow alone. There was no longer the protective buffer he felt in Mary's handling the door. The younger people who began working the line allowed more to go unchallenged. At times he felt betrayed by this, the sensitive, gentle man that he was. He began drinking more, and his "holidays" became extended.

Still, he loved his work to the end. The last meal he prepared was the morning feast on Christmas Day. He wore multicolored bowling shoes while he worked. He loved red shirts, and wore his pants a bit too high. His walk was a shuffle of feet, his cadence something akin to a galleon gliding into bay. In warm weather he and Sal would sit for hours in front of the house. And at the table, his place in one corner of the dining room had a quiet all its own.

Although he sometimes felt uncomprehended by the younger volunteers, John had an openness to them that was unmatched. He was ever solicitous of those he thought had come to truly work rather than take advantage. His was a certain tenderness and interest not common to most around the house, and a friendship that could be inspiring. Whiskers said he came back to New York because of John McMullan. John received letters from friends all over the country. One, Dana LaRose O'Brien, sent him a mug from Ireland this summer.

John did not become old. He liked contemporary music, and on one occasion bought the Beatles' record "Let It Be" because it fit his philosophy. His generosity went beyond cigarettes. He would share the little extras a Catholic Worker cook can manage with this person or that, a sandwich now and then or an egg and fried potatoes. He always made sure Dorothy had some of the canned milk for her coffee in the morning. And when he finally had a check coming in for the disability following a leg operation, he would put some of it out to get this one on a bus to sobriety in Philadelphia, or send a brother in Ireland seed money for the farm.

John had his Irish, too, a vein of belligerence that could be gotten up. To sit in his chair was to learn it shouldn't be done. To criticize his cooking was to be unwelcomed. He had no tolerance for loafers, what he called "Catholic Shirkers." He also had a curious vanity for appearance and would gather sacks of clothing, some of which went for sale when in a pinch.

Red, like his face in laughter, was his favorite color. But I would have to say that blue dominated this rather private person. It was his customary dress. There was a reserve, a just pride, a propriety about him. Like so many alcoholics, there were hidden sorrows locked deep within him, and these served to make him warm but somewhat distant. He understood others who were walking the line and would give them his own brand of encouragement. His friendship had a gratuitous quality that did not attach strings, but "Let be."

John had had trouble with steps for years. He had bad ankles, perhaps from a previous accident, and we used to watch him when he'd go up to bed. (He had moved into the fourth floor a year and a half ago, following hospitalization for varicose veins.) The night after Christmas he slipped while coming down for supper from the top step on the second landing. He plunged the full flight, fracturing his cervical spine and suffering a complete paralysis. After ten days, he succumbed, dying on the Feast of the Epiphany.

Those ten days were days of grace. As Kathleen said, he seemed to live them for us, enduring merely on will. Many came to visit him, including his sister. He could not speak but could move his lips. One of the first things he communicated when he regained consciousness was "I'm all right, I'll be OK." This was characteristic of John. As in life, so in death. He did not wish others to be overly anxious for him. Several times he asked for a smoke, but of course, he was attached to an oxygen machine! And his eyes smiled when we told him the line was having extra turkey because we'd been given so many this year. He suffered perhaps three cardiac arrests, the final one the most telling. He was anointed and expertly cared for up to the end.

Father Lyle conducted the funeral Mass. It was said on the table where John had made so many bowls of soup, cut so many carrots and parsnips, peeled so many onions. John must have been standing there in his usual manner, arms extending down to the top of the table. Among us were tears, Rachel uncomforted, weeping for her children. And, once more, the words of Hopkins, read at the liturgy:

> Each mortal thing does one thing and the same:
>
> . . . Crying Whát I dó is me: for that I came.
> I say móre: the just man justices;
> Keeps grace: that keeps all his goings graces;
> Acts in God's eye what in God's eye he is—
> Christ. For Christ plays in ten thousand places,
> Lovely in limbs, and lovely in eyes not his
> To the Father through the features of men's faces.

Joseph Johnston
Our Gentleman Friend

BY DAVID BESEDA

The Catholic Worker October–November 1982

A FEW DAYS AGO, Joseph Johnston left behind his failing body to join with the saints, and so we have lost our gentleman of Maryhouse. For awhile, Joe had the distinction of being the only man in a house full of forty women. Even at seventy-six years old, he rose to the privilege of such a situation by treating all women with the same charm and old-worldly ways that must have formerly won the heart of his wife, Rose. Joe and Rose first came to the Catholic Worker about five years ago, when a social worker sent this elderly couple for "only one night" of emergency hospitality. As so often happens, we couldn't find a nursing home who would take them as a couple, and so they settled into Maryhouse.

I first met Joe three years ago, on the sad day Rose died of a stroke. In a very touching expression of his sorrow, Joe just kept repeating, "I've lost the love of my life, my only sweetheart." Shortly afterwards, Joe and I became roommates, and for some time Joe used to tell me that his wife often came down from heaven to visit him. He said it with such sincerity that I always expected to walk in and find her hovering in our room.

Joe always spoke of heaven with such certainty that it stunned me, and I felt then that I was seeing in his eyes, the eternal. Because of a dislocated hip, Joe had to use a metal walker to move around and one day he asked me, so as to prepare himself, "I won't need this walker when I go to heaven, will I?" I didn't remind him that some people say there are stairways to heaven, for Joe had paid his dues in struggling each day to get his walker and sore leg up and down about fifty Maryhouse steps.

Joe liked to spend his days sitting on the landing at the top of our first set of stairs—checking out the front door, and munching on sugar-powdered jelly donuts that Helen, Johanna, or others would bring to him. Joe always appreciated the house and the care he received (although bad meals or locked bathrooms sent him shouting and rattling his walker). But he confided to me one day that he had his doubts about the place, since there seemed to be mostly women in the "army barracks" with him. Joe had served in awful battle situations, so he figured the army would always take care of him. In trying to understand Maryhouse, then, he associated it with the life in the military which he knew so well. I didn't try to explain that we were trying to be a pacifist community, because to him our life seemed just like the army; for example, army food is usually bad, army pay is low, army men suffer injuries and march up and down a lot.

But if Joe was confused about some things, he was very clear in his understanding that God would make things better for him. He attended Mass in the house regularly, and in his last days he prayed and waited for the time to come. We love him and miss him and will remember him, but we give thanks that this man, who was such a gentleman, and a friend to us all, has now entered eternal life.

Earl Ovitt

BY PATRICK JORDAN

The Catholic Worker December 1984

EARL OVITT, WHO FOR some two decades has shared his vast abilities and generous person with members of the New York Catholic Worker, died at the end of this year's long Labor Day weekend. His great heart, overburdened with punishing, nearly compulsive work and the disregard of one who treats all others more kindly than oneself, suddenly succumbed.

For those of us who were honored to know his love and presence, who had seen Earl pass practically unscathed through many physically perilous episodes before, there was little surprise, but profound shock and loss. And while we shall always treasure our friendship and the reassurance that one so unique and special as Earl is welcomed most immediately and graciously into Christ's embrace, it will always be with the bittersweet recognition that we ourselves were never able to satisfy and set in equilibrium his heart's vast desires. The peace he so rightly deserved, we were not able to give. Yet despite that, and to the end, Earl was always understanding of us, and rich in friendship toward us. He did everything with a vigor and humanity that seemed boundless in capacity. And only now is he or could he be set free by the One Who is the Fullness of All Desire.

In the time that we knew him, Earl Ovitt was the consummate jack-of-all-trades. His abilities were equalled only by his generous responsiveness. What he did not have by way of tool or solution, he would invent. He knew buildings from foundation to capstone, from water routes to wiring. He looked at repair problems with a diagnostic genius, and seemed to know the hidden nature of a structure as if by radiology. He conveyed his solutions to those who might be assisting him, in a discourse so technical and laden with carpenter's terminology that often his assistant felt utterly at sea, only to experience, as well, the underriding hand of Earl's confidence and direction so fully at work that it brought them both to the project's resounding fulfillment and achievement. In this sense he was a master teacher. He was always impressing others with the assurance that: "That's not too hard . . . You can get that done easily by . . ." and then giving the person all the plans, tools, and imagination necessary to achieve the needed repair.

He was as solid and stalwart as his Vermont roots. His mind was ever probing for the historical context of a given event. He read the daily paper with the keenness of an archivist, and was always bringing choice slices of information to the person particularly in need of such insights. His vocabulary was a tribute to one whose self-education never stops. And he could laugh so hard the tears would roll down his cheeks. He was one of those people who could not only discern the humorous event, but could construct it afterwards in such a way as to evoke laughter from others.

All these attributes would be enough to make him a remarkably attractive person, but there was more: physical strength and comeliness; a love of music (he composed his own songs) and movement (the great bands danced in his blood); a loyalty to friends and country; and an uncommon gentleness that was seen not only in his gentlemanliness, but in his care for children, for fellow sufferers, for animals, for flowers and vegetable plants, the latter of which he took great pride in cultivating each year at his little cottage on Staten Island. He was, we can testify, generous beyond reckoning.

There was a dark side to Earl as well—the crucifixion element that is shared so deeply by many of those drawn into Catholic Worker communities. It is the adamant of suffering which is at the heart of our fallen nature. Yet it is the searing fire of honesty and judgment that are the birthplace of a compassion which proves to be the gate of heaven. Earl well knew this. In fact, he was something of a sign of it. At hellish intervals he would sink into an all too unbecoming debasement. Yet, even then his spirit was uncommonly generous to those who shared affliction, like those remarkable melodies born out of the depths of tragic opera.

It was no surprise that many friends and family came to celebrate Earl's life at the memorial Mass held at St. Joseph's House on the Feast of Our Lady of Sorrows. We came with sorrow, but our singing that night was born of profound gratitude. For through such companions as Earl we all know the truth of Scripture: "You spare all things, because they are Yours, O Lord, lover of souls; and Your imperishable spirit is in them all!" (Wisdom 11:27–12:1)

Harold Henry Gay

BY GARY DONATELLI

The Catholic Worker September 1985

HAROLD, BY SELF-DEFINITION, WAS a senior citizen and an artist, said his daily prayers, and had just as much right to live here as any of these other devil-minded troublemakers. That's right! Every day he would go across the street to the Spanish-American grocery store and get a pint of ice cream to bring back and eat. Without fail, he would check the coffee urn for coffee each time he came down to the first floor, regardless of the time of day. Then he'd find a seat and smoke a cigarette, or maybe first find a cigarette, bend over and light it under the urn and then find a seat. You could often find Harold up on the second floor watching the Silvertone television set, or some days he'd walk over to the old music school building (Maryhouse) to listen to a "record recording machine" that they have in the dining room there.

Harold had a great deal of respect for certain individuals and their family relations, and absolutely no respect for certain other individuals, if you wanted to know. He would often tell us so, whether we wanted to know or not. Years ago, Harold used to write letters to anybody he thought was doing a good job: popes, politicians, entertainers, heads of corporations, health care workers, Catholic Workers. He was also one for greeting cards, which he was always sure to get out early: Thanksgiving cards by mid-October, Christmas cards just before Thanksgiving, Easter cards before you had begun to reconcile yourself to Lent. For Harold, respect was a serious business.

We're not exactly sure when Harold came to the Catholic Worker, but by 1968, when we moved to 36 East First Street, Harold was around. He lived in the flophouses on the Bowery, kept the second floor clean, decorated the fire escape among other things, and drank his fair share of cheap wine. The fire escape was a delight back then; there was a wooden cross that would constantly change and evolve as Harold would find assorted ribbons, tape, plastic flowers, stuffed animals, etc., to add to or replace what had weathered. One of his more famous cleaning projects was when he was asked to clean out the kitchenette on the second floor, and he ripped up about half of the back issues of *The Catholic Worker* that had been stored there, before someone noticed what he was doing.

One very cold February night, Harold disappeared. We called the hospitals and checked the morgue, to no avail. A few months later, downtown Beekman Hospital called, saying they had a Mr. Gay there who said he knew us. The police apparently found him on the street that freezing February night, and brought him to the hospital. He had a temperature of 80 degrees. I often wondered if, after that, Harold was never the same, or merely more of the same. At any rate, Harold was discharged and, after respectfully thanking the hospital staff, came to live at St. Joseph House, where he maintained a highly visible or maybe even more audible presence. Harold had a lot to say; ask anyone who spent any time living on the third floor, or anyone who had tried to watch the Silvertone television set up on the second floor, or anyone who had tried to say Vespers in the evening on the first floor, or anyone who had walked through the door of the house. Harold was easy to overhear, and hence, hard to overlook. His monologues and stories were part of our day-in, day-out lives; something we accepted usually without thinking about it, unless on occasion when he could sufficiently distract, irritate, or drown out ten or so pious Vespers sayers, or it was two in the morning on the third floor and Harold was just starting to warm up. But more often, he'd give us occasion to smile, laugh, or even applaud, in which case he would respectfully acknowledge our ovation, and then maybe dance back to his chair or towards the stairs and make an exit. Some of us thought he had been an entertainer in a former life. He certainly had a flair for the theatrical, but after all, he was an artist, you know.

One Sunday morning, early in August, Harold quietly checked out of our lives and our house. We gathered in the summer heat on a grassy hillside in Calvary Cemetery to bury our friend. We said our prayers without interruption this time. The grave diggers lowered his body into the grave (very respectfully, I thought), and we quietly returned to and piled into the van and station wagon, and drove away to the noisy roar of a little bulldozer which they used to fill in Harold's grave.

Gary Leib

BY BILL GRIFFIN

The Catholic Worker March–April 1986

ALBERT CAMUS PRAISED THE writer Louis Guilloux for the restraint and re-serve of his books that dealt with the lives of the poor. Guilloux had struck the right balance, according to Camus, for to say too much would be a further insult to their dignity and to say too little would be a final betrayal of the hard truth of their lives. Bearing this admonition in mind, I want to attempt to write a few words about Gary Leib.

Gary's death was tragic and dramatic. He was a young man, only thirty-eight years old. He suffered from severe alcoholism. He lived in the streets for the most part, shunning the Municipal Men's Shelter as many do because it is an overcrowded, impersonal, and often physically violent place. For more than twelve years he had been a regular visitor at St. Joseph House, coming for a winter coat or for some soup and coffee. Gary sought out the Catholic Worker, surely, out of necessity when he was in dire straits and it was below freezing outside, but some ineffable affection for the place drew him as well. His family brought gifts to the Worker that were passed on to Gary when he was not drinking.

During the last several years, the alcoholism took an increasing toll on him; he began to have grand mal seizures. Three or so years ago his leg was broken and he had to wear a cast for many months. During the last two years, his mental state deteriorated to the point where he could barely verbalize his basic needs. One day early in February of this year, after suffering a seizure at St. Joseph House, he was brought up to Bellevue Hospital in an ambulance. For some reason Gary left the emergency room, wandered from the building, and fell into an excavation site nearby. Perhaps he then had another seizure. It was bitterly cold that night and Gary froze to death.

The terrible irony of his death on the grounds of a hospital attracted the attention of the media, and people from *Newsday* appeared at St. Joseph House in search of more detail. The microcosm of the Catholic Worker's daily effort to provide food and shelter for the poor of the Lower East Side suddenly became part of the macrocosm of our national and municipal response to the plight of the homeless. The inference that was drawn from Gary's death during a later radio broadcast was, I gather, that the needs of the homeless are not being met. The story quickly faded from public attention.

There is an aspect of this tragedy that has not been addressed as yet. I would like to bring it out and make a contribution to understanding it more fully in this eulogy for Gary. During the winter and spring of 1985, working as a registered nurse on the neurology/neurosurgery floor of Bellevue Hospital, I happened to be present for three of Gary's hospitalizations. Let me describe what I saw Gary go through as a sick man and a homeless man.

Gary received excellent medical care while in the hospital. The first time I saw him at Bellevue he was having a seizure. No effort was spared to try to stabilize him and then discover the exact cause of his convulsions. Blood cultures, X-rays, CAT scans, spinal taps, indeed the whole wondrous array of modern diagnostic tools was called into service. Medical thought currently attributes alcoholic seizures to the chemical additives in wine and/or the continuous head trauma sustained from falls while intoxicated. Fortunately, most seizures can be controlled by abstinence and the use of anticonvulsants such as Dilantin and phenobarbital.

After a four-week stay, Gary was free from seizures and more coherent. He could give no home address; there was no alternative but to discharge him to the Men's Shelter. Out he went with a bottle of Dilantin capsules, a prescription, instructions to return for a doctor's appointment in a week, and a subway token. I saw him a few days later on the soup line. He was drinking. After receiving a meal he returned to the street.

Several months later, I saw Gary at Bellevue again. This time his condition was much more serious. Not only was he suffering from seizures, but his jaw was broken and he had increased intracranial pressure. The cerebrospinal fluid which bathes the brain was not draining; this was put down to head trauma. Gary had to undergo a craniotomy in which a shunt, a newly invented, very thin, plastic draining tube was placed in a ventricle of his brain to draw off the excess fluid. The invention of this shunt has saved the lives of many children suffering from hydrocephaly.

Postoperatively, Gary had to receive intravenous antibiotics around the clock for a period of weeks. His jaws were wired shut to promote healing. He had to be fed high-protein liquids through a tube and, when that was removed, he had to drink everything through a straw. A tremendous surgical and nursing effort was devoted to Gary's care by the hospital staff. Gary improved markedly and was able to verbalize much more. "Hey, Bill, you still down at the Worker?" he asked once out of the blue after days of silence.

When his recovery was complete, he was again discharged to the Municipal Shelter with the same disastrous results. Within hours he was under the influence and asking for a meal at St. Joseph House. In the days that followed, yogurts and puddings were provided for him when he came by for meals. The Catholic Worker had neither the workers nor the space to take on the responsibility for Gary's full-time care. People there befriended Gary as they could; John Carter was especially concerned about his welfare.

Because he was young and had a strong constitution, Gary survived his trials that winter, but at a great price. He lost a good deal of weight and he became progressively less coherent. His sense of balance became impaired and he had difficulty walking.

I saw Gary for a third time last summer at Bellevue. Again it was an emergency admission for seizure activity. He stayed for another several weeks in the hospital; his jaw healed in the meantime and the wires were removed. Again he was discharged when he was stable to the Men's Shelter, which "is another way of saying to the street, because I know he won't stay there," a social worker assigned to Gary told me in frustration. "There are just no long-term residential care facilities for people like Gary," she added sadly.

The tragic atmosphere of wasted effort surrounds Gary and this is the aspect of his story that has not been addressed and that needs to be understood more fully. The disease of alcoholism, combined with the onset of seizures and all the pressures of being a homeless man, assured that Gary would return repeatedly to the hospital. Gary had numerous other hospitalizations besides the ones I witnessed and have described.

When I speak of waste I do not want to suggest in any way whatsoever that the medical care Gary received ought not to have been given. My point is exactly the contrary; I contend that Gary did receive enough care. If there had existed some long-term residential care facility, a place staffed with compassionate people, at some distance, at least, from the Bowery, a place where Gary could have been taken in and followed medically, then I am certain many of his hospitalizations could have been avoided.

A hospital bed costs $500 a day at Bellevue; add to that the cost of the medications, of the delicate operation, of the constant nursing care. At a rough estimate, each of Gary's stays in the hospital that I have spoken of cost about $20,000. This was never wasted on Gary, but the final goal of all this expense and hard work, Gary's recovery and health, was put out of reach for want of proper housing and continued medical support. Many good efforts bore no fruit; this is what is terrible. More terrible still is the thought of the physical suffering Gary might have been saved if some of his hospitalizations had not been necessary.

For the person of faith, the last word, if there can be one in such a situation, must come from the mystery at the heart of every life. Gary was a gentle and generous man. From him we receive the precious knowledge that our attempts to help the homeless are woefully inadequate and inconsistent. We can provide for emergency hospitalization and technologically sophisticated operations on the human brain; but we are unable as yet to provide a fellow human being with appropriate shelter right after such interventions. Gary's sufferings give him grandeur; they can bring us wisdom. We must pray to receive and to act on this wisdom which is Gary's great gift to us.

Michael Malinowski

The Catholic Worker April 1986

ON WALKS WITH DEANE, when I hear the farm dogs barking excitedly behind us, rushing to catch up in anticipation of a good long walk, I think
of Mike. I think of Mike because I know they're not thinking of us, but of
him. He was a man who knew how to keep a dog's love—undivided and
faithful for life. The dogs know he's gone but they still expect the walks, the
good long walks along the path to the hayfields. Mike is gone. He's been
"promoted to glory," as Joe is fond of saying.

"Old Man" Mike, as we affectionately dubbed him, lived in the green
house with Arthur, George, Slim, and more recently, Joe. Arthur and Mike,
more than the others, were a household. But above all they were friends.
And yet they were very different. They divided up the chores evenly: Arthur
cooked and kept the peace. Mike kept the house clean.

Mike came to Peter Maurin Farm four years ago at the age of seventy-nine. He was living at St. Joseph House when we at the farm began
to hear of him. A plot was hatched to settle him at the farm, a scheme to
which Mike readily assented, as he had lived in the Catskills in earlier
years, and loved the country. And so the last years of his life were spent in
contentment with his new family, bound to him not by ties of blood but
those of mutual acceptance.

It wasn't long before he had found his niche. In the summer he mowed
the lawn. Slow in his movements and gnarled as an old tree, he was inde-
fatigable. We used to joke with him, saying he'd outlive us all. And because
he kept the grounds around the house so neat and trim, we'd sometimes rib
him about how people would mistake us for suburbanites if he kept it up.

Mike liked to garden, and enjoyed working with others. He and Arthur kept a flower garden overflowing with masses of nasturtiums and marigolds, and redolent of cosmos and sweetpeas climbing up the porch supports. (He was especially proud of the sweetpeas.) If farm work was in progress it was a sure bet that Mike would appear and lend a hand or offer us some choice piece of wisdom on the subject. In almost any endeavor we were engaged in he would help, whether it was planting, hoeing, harvesting, or chopping wood. He was, indeed, a real apologist of good old-fashioned hard work, and found many opportunities to expound on this theme.

With a twinkle in his eye and a ready "aw'right" to encourage us, he'd set to work and entertain us with anecdotes of his merchant seaman days. He was fond of telling how he had traveled around the world and would tease us with some unblushing sea stories, like the one about his wife in every port.

Mike's greatest anchor to the farm, however, was Chuck. He and Chuck were more than master and dog. They were buddies. In fact, Chuck is the only dog in Catholic Worker history, to my knowledge, to occupy a people-sized bed all of his own. And yet it was enough to see the loving glow in Mike's eye to understand how this could be. Towards the end, during Mike's long illness, after he was taken to Rosary Hill (a hospice for the terminally ill in Hawthorne, New York, run by the Hawthorne Dominican sisters) Chuck would, on occasion, come visit Mike with us, jumping up on the bed, whining with joy and licking his dying friend's face.

Mike had cancer; in keeping with its insidious nature, it was a long time incubating. One day in September Mike complained of a searing pain in his throat. He blamed the rice crispies he'd had for breakfast. One must have lodged in his throat. But the doctor found something else. Mike was immediately admitted to St. Luke's Hospital in Newburgh. A week later the surgeons removed his larynx. From then on Mike was forced to write his thoughts to us. He would never speak again. Later, chemotherapy was tried with poor results.

Despite these setbacks, Mike rallied us, grinning his determination and pumping the air with his fists to let us know he wasn't giving up just yet. He did not know that the cancer had spread to his lymph system and now riddled his body. Still, he was determined to come home and so he did, only to say goodbye to the farm for good. A few days later he was back in the hospital and arrangements were made to prepare a place for him at Rosary Hill.

Surrounded by the immaculate and prayerful serenity of the hospice, and the gentle, loving care of the orderlies and the sisters, who treated him not like a patient but like a suffering comrade, Mike settled himself to wait for death. His thoughts turned increasingly heavenward, and as he grew weaker and less able to communicate, he'd sometimes, after a long pause, slowly raise his arm and point to the ceiling. The eyes following the arm would then turn back toward us, asparkle with joy. Then, with an eloquence that no words could equal, he'd bring his old gnarled hands together in an attitude of prayer.

Mike left us on the thirty-first of January. I remember it as a brilliantly clear and cold morning with the sun just beginning to tint the horizon. I wanted to laugh and dance knowing he is free and happy now as he never was before. Instead, I wore the customary long face that death requires. His body we buried in St. Mary's Cemetery, Marlboro, just behind the farm; but as for where Mike really is, there is no doubt in my mind.

Johanna
Artist: M. Eileen Lawter

Johanna

BY KATHARINE TEMPLE

The Catholic Worker December 1986

JOHANNA DIED SUDDENLY ON the Sunday before Advent. The morning of her burial, I walked into the dining room to hear, "By tradition, today is the day we rush out to start Christmas shopping!" The words and tone were jarring. Not fully taking it in as a radio advertisement, I thought to myself, "Really, what does this have to do with anything? And anyway, in Christian tradition, we're moving into Advent and not right to Christmas." I can't help but wonder whether, in Johanna's life and death, we haven't been given a quite different sign for the season of waiting and hope.

St. Augustine once said that hope is given only to the humble, and maybe this is what Johanna can teach us, for she was completely anonymous in the grand scheme of pomp and circumstance. She had known deep suffering throughout her life and had defied that brokenness by refusing to give in, despite all evidence to the contrary. She was, in her own way, in the *status viatoris*, the state of being on the way to the Kingdom that has not yet fully come. And such a state, whether her hope was conscious or unconscious, supernatural or a tactic for survival, is the very stuff, the traditional definition of Christian hope.

Early on in Advent, while reading the passage from Isaiah 3 that says, "On that day the Lord will take away the finery," and goes on to list "the festal robes, the mantles, the cloaks, and the purses," I immediately thought of Johanna. The day she died there was *nothing* personal in her room, except for half a package of Top tobacco. She had been stripped of everything: her job, home, friends, family, and, finally, her mind. As an outward sign, she stripped herself of all possessions, all superfluous conversation, the clothes she had worn so beautifully, and often food and drink. She moved, instead, to live more and more within herself, with a certain grace even, interspersed with outbursts of rage. In this way, she refused to succumb completely to the despair within or to the false conditions and therapeutic definitions without. She watched and she waited, she suffered and railed, she did not accept the crumbs of consolation offered. In this way, too, she reminded me of a contemporary Job.

Johanna's life was not the fullness of what God wants for His children. It is hard to fathom how she lived in any hope, seemingly so often without the hope that is "the shoot, and the bud of the bloom of eternity itself" (Charles Péguy). As Arturo said to me after the funeral, "The hardest thing to bear is that Johanna did not live to see the Kingdom arrive." And yet, her life was not in vain either, for she had a holiness, the hidden face of God almost, that longs for the new Creation more than anything else. As we start a new Church year, not with the presence of God, but waiting for His hidden arrival as the Child, we should ponder these things in our hearts. At the graveside, we pleaded as much for ourselves as for Johanna, when we prayed that she might be fully restored when she sees God face to face.

BY CANDY CLARKE

IT SOMEHOW SEEMS A betrayal, my writing words to describe Johanna's life with us, knowing that these will end up printed in our newspaper, for Johanna's way of expressing herself was with few spoken words. Instead, a bandage often over her mouth, a coat pulled up over her head, a gauze pad taped over one eye, her ever erect posture, her entrance into the kitchen (when it was nearly empty of folks) to see what there was in the pantry or on the table so as to decide what little she'd partake of—all of these and more were a revelation to those of us who would take the time (of which there always seems to be so little) to see and accept Johanna "as she was."

Not to say that she was averse to words—so often she would be seen with a stubby pencil in hand, writing on matchcovers or paper she would find in the office. Jane, one of our historians (longevity around here gets you this title), told me Johanna was known to use a spare typewriter over at St. Joseph House where she first came to stay.

But we never saw this writing. Johanna lived a most austere life (most of the rest of us either collect clothes or books—Johanna did neither), disposing of all that she wrote. With her non-verbalness, it was an easy assumption to make that she lived in "another world." But with the help of the collective memories of others I now know of or can remember myself, a real connectedness Johanna had with the world around her. Her tucking Mary O'Connor into bed at night in the early days of Maryhouse; her joy and spiritedness when a Catholic Worker couple brought their infant to visit and let Johanna hold the child. One day quite recently, when I warned her she might want to avoid the adjacent hallway for awhile since someone else was doing one of her "volcanic eruptions," Johanna replied, "You don't suppose she's lost her Actor's Equity [union] card?"

She had lived in Maryhouse as long as the latter has been open. We hope our memories of her will help keep alive our history of these past ten or eleven years.

In recent times, she most often stayed around the house, frequently ascending or descending the three flights of stairs to and from her room, perhaps liking being an observer (rather than a participant) from an alcove off the dining room, where the action usually is (if there is any). She ate so very little, having difficulty accepting anything from others. Going to local stores was hard on her—her "differentness" was not easily accepted by others. It was then that I could see her anger, something she rarely showed.

I remember, once, bringing up the thought of counseling or medication to her, to which she did not acquiesce. To this day, I do not know if we should've forced the issue. We chose instead to let Johanna decide.

Please, Lord, grant us forgiveness for what we did or did not do, have Johanna know of our concern, our love, and our gratitude for her lessons to us in how to listen. Thank you, Johanna, for sharing your life with us all, and teaching us how to be present to the God Who dwells within each of us.

Elinore Hayes

BY KATHARINE TEMPLE

The Catholic Worker October–November 1987

"ELINORE, THE STRIFE IS o'er, the battle done," was the last thing I said to her in the hospital. They were also the words Jane greeted me with to tell me Elinore had died, and the hymn we sang at her burial in Calvary Cemetery.

Her life—at least as much as we knew over the past fifteen or so years, with only elusive hints about earlier times—was racked with pain and disappointment, as well as a valiant struggle against all the odds. We knew that, all of us who were sitting around talking and reminiscing in the time-honored fashion after a funeral. Each favorite story began with a battle royal from "Lady Elinore" (as Mark Samara used to address her): Elinore's rants when she couldn't come in because of her drinking; flamboyant scenes with neighbors on Second Avenue; well-aimed disruptions of a Friday Night Meeting, like the time she swayed into a panel discussion on homelessness and opined in loud, ringing tones, "I don't know whether this is diarrhea of the mouth or constipation of the mind"; Frank and me removing her from one such occasion, even though we half agreed; more often than not a tale about an encounter when someone first arrived at the house. I'll never forget my first run-in. Full of lofty principles, the new person on the scene, I made the mistake one evening of standing too long at the tea urn in the middle of the dining room. Elinore spied me and pounced with, "You think your so f——— smart, but you're not kind!" Later, all I could think was, "Truer words were never spoken."

Sometimes the cry of pain, a pronouncement of wrath, her voice of judgment, was all that people heard. All of us who were mourning, though, were not remembering just the outbursts: One of the desert fathers said that "prayer demands constant combat to the last breath," but for her it would probably go the other way around. Her combat was a form of prayer, you might say, to demand perfection.

(Caution: I can just picture Elinore reading this out loud, with a snort of laughter, as she used to comb the paper to find references to her friends and also to expose our pretensions. Too bad she'll miss such a golden opportunity now.)

But, of course, to imagine Elinore as a desert mother is a bit far-fetched. After all, she was not exactly a hermit, nor was she known for long periods of silence. She was more like a matriarch, an Athena, the goddess both of battle and the hearth. If each story started with a fight, the ending was always some sort of setting things to right. If you survived the initial onslaught, sooner or later Elinore made up for it and initiated you into the family. In my case, she later told me I looked like Jane Wyman—a dubious fabrication, but a restoration of good humor and peace in the household nevertheless.

Yes, Elinore, you demanded, as only a mother can, that we *be* the family we go on and on about. You never let us get away with anything. You kept our feet on the ground. You overturned all the stereotypes about host(esses) and guests in a house of hospitality and any notions of artificial structure. In an environment of isolation and individualism, you forged the family ties that bind.

As Michael Harank reminded us in his beautiful eulogy at the funeral Mass on August 17, her suffering was not only her own suffering. He spoke of her deep feeling for the sufferings of others; her great love of beauty (through which, Dostoevsky tells us, the world will be saved); her solitude, which found expression in a favorite poem, Wordsworth's "Daffodils"; and her kindnesses over the years. Above all, she was faithful in the little things that go to expel the long loneliness. Without fail, she persisted as the guardian of birthdays and anniversaries, sending personal notes of affection on each one. Even when she was confined to bed with crippling arthritis and gout, she followed avidly the paths of those who have left the houses and wanted to know every detail of how they and their children were faring. She insisted on a sense of propriety (no matter that she herself was often the immediate source of chaos!) and respect for everyone, starting with Miss Day, whose loss she never ceased to grieve, and extending to anyone she felt was getting lost in the shuffle.

Yes, in your own inimitable way, you wrestled your way to be the barren woman who returned home as the mother of children (Psalm 113:9). (For some reason, in modern Hebrew the word for "barren woman" can also mean "mainstay." A strange combination, which when I first heard it, brought Elinore to mind.) You knew what the Catholic Worker was supposed to be all about.

(Another caution: There is a temptation to relegate Elinore to tales from "the good old days," stories designed mainly to make us feel good about ourselves. That would make her furious.)

Nothing became Elinore's life like the leaving of it. For several months, ending up with seven weeks in the intensive care unit, she had to be in Bellevue Hospital. It was certainly a time of deep suffering for a woman who never wanted doctors or medicine, who rejected any form of impersonal charity, who hated to be fenced in, who railed against the thought she might be deserted, who both dreaded and desired death in what looked like a cosmic struggle. Deane, in her wisdom, has said that Elinore's whole life was a form of purgatory on earth, and her last weeks were the culmination of her purifying suffering.

Such was her stamina that her body constantly resisted the physical and emotional and spiritual assaults on it. Whenever I saw her in the ICU, it seemed to me that, at a great price, she had been given time to conquer her demons. In the words of the same hymn, "Death's mightiest powers have done their worst." Towards the end, the raging subsided as she moved to accept all the technical ministrations of the medical team with no little grace, and to receive "the Elinore troops" (so named by one of the doctors), the various acquaintances who did not desert her, but came to comfort and be comforted by her. In her own words, with an admittedly un-Pauline twist and tone, she kept the faith, baby, to the end.

Now that she was gone before us, buried with Anna Zukas, another Maryhouse matriarch, in the family plot of Sister Renée, whom Elinor loved so deeply, we can include her with confidence on November 1, when we sing, "For all the saints, who from their labors rest."

Linda Cruickshank

BY MEG HYRE

The Catholic Worker March–April 1988

ON FRIDAY EVENING, THE fifth of February, Linda Cruickshank died in Bellevue Hospital, while I was with her, ending more than a year of illness and months of extreme hardship and suffering. Linda was thirty-seven years old. We believe that she was born in Baltimore, Maryland, and no one really knows how she came to New York from there. Linda came to the Catholic Worker about fifteen years ago.

I had heard while in England that Linda was very ill, most probably with AIDS, although she would not submit to testing. One afternoon last October, shortly after my return home, I was going into the house when her voice at my elbow said, "Hello, Meg." I turned around in shock, because I had seen her on my way in, but so changed was she that I had taken her, with her jacket hood up, to be a man I didn't know. Her face was haggard and her complexion literally grey. She had come to the house to ask Marylin to take her up to the hospital. I met Marylin on the stairs and offered to come with them, since it was sure to be a long wait. Marylin welcomed the company, and added, with words which could have set the seal on the next four months: "Long wait? It's a vigil—we'll be there all night." And so we were, from five p.m. to five a.m., when Linda was finally admitted.

It is no exaggeration to say that for the poor, this is a city in crisis; and one sees that nowhere more clearly than in the emergency rooms, clinics, and wards of the city hospitals. Nowhere (with the undoubted exception of the prisons and the shelters) does one witness more acutely the shattered bodies and spirits of the permanently dispossessed. To be homeless is almost inevitably to be chronically ill. The suffering of so many of these people is an inexorable movement toward a cruel death; they absorb with their own flesh the daily violence of this world, and have no out. This is the death that was Linda's.

That first purgatorial sojourn in the emergency room up at Bellevue merges unclearly into one with all of those which followed. Sitting up the night on slippery plastic chairs under the fluorescent lights and thinking that even in jail, one could lie down on the concrete floor to sleep. Here, police passed through at irregular hours to awaken any who had laid their heads down, including the sick who were not on stretchers, and to send away any who were just seeking a place out of the cold. Linda lay on a stretcher with her head under the covers, blown upon first by a sweltering hot heating vent, then by chill drafts as the double doors of the ER opened and closed. She slept through the din by force of exhaustion, and tolerated the place only because she lacked the strength to walk out. In the overflowing emergency room, she waited some twenty-four hours before a bed was available for her. Another time, the wait was closer to three days. More than once, she waited but was not admitted because the hospital was so overtaxed that—in the absence of acute complications—to be dying and barely able to stand could not merit her a bed.

In the beginning, I was vexed and exasperated by Linda's way of signing herself out of the hospital as soon as she had the strength to do so. This difficulty was compounded by her frequent lack of cooperation with those who were trying to care for her—refusing IVs by pulling them out; refusing tests that would confirm that she had HIV, and therefore admit her to the network of services provided by the city for people with AIDS; coughing and spitting indiscriminately; demanding what she needed in a way that could make others just not want to hear about it. These things led to her being even more neglected than she would have been otherwise, simply as someone without the strength and lucidity to manage matters more tactfully. Sheets might go unchanged, medicine unadministered, or food ungiven because the overburdened staff would refuse or not be able to attend to such a difficult patient.

To make matters worse, Linda's departures from the hospital brought her back to the doorstep of the Catholic Worker, where we were fast feeling caught between our inability to give her the sort of care she needed and our unwillingness to consign her as winter approached to the streets or the shelters. Technically speaking, she did make a choice when she left the hospital despite warnings that we couldn't care for her in the houses. But at

52

the deeper level, given the brutality of it all, "choice" had no real meaning, and we all knew that, too. Finally, arrangements were worked out whereby Linda could sleep overnight at Maryhouse and spend the days at St. Joseph House. For the rest of it, we could only take her to the hospital when she felt the absolute need, and receive her back again, until the time when she would enter the hospital but never have the strength to leave it. That happened in the last week of December.

This time Linda didn't regain strength, despite rest and a blood transfusion. She was seldom able to take even her favorite drinks—the root beer that her visitors brought her and the egg nog that her doctor ordered for her daily. She gave up the word games and puzzles of which she had been a devotee, no longer having the concentration for them. How long she might persevere in this way was anyone's guess—but efforts to make an application to Bailey House (a fine residence here in Manhattan for homeless people with AIDS) were quietly set aside, and the social workers began to think in terms of a state nursing home instead. This was a process we did nothing to expedite, believing that her care would not be much improved elsewhere, but that she might be sent too far away for daily visits.

By now, I had come to a much different view of Linda's earlier "elopements" and continuing nonconformity with the hospital regimen. Over the weeks it had been impressed on me that Linda was operating on a different and more urgent plane of existence than the rest of us who were trying to reason with her about her need for hospital care, the vagaries of the social services system, etc. I understood it for the first time one day when I arrived at the hospital just after Linda had signed herself out. As I stepped out of the elevator, a figure at the far end of the hall caught my eye. Instinctively, I turned to take a better look at the unmistakable grace of this dark and slender apparition. I took in the vision of long-limbed beauty for one more second before realizing that this was Linda, still draped in her hospital gown, strolling the corridor with her IV apparatus on one hand and her cigarette in the other. She was still a desperately ill woman, but I understood then that the fullness of life that was left in her would take every chance it was given to shine forth.

I sat beside her on her bed, asking her not to leave the hospital, telling her there was no guarantee that she could come back to the Worker to stay. I was unfairly aggravated because I did not look forward to coping with the inevitable dilemma once again; but even so, her point of view was starting to make sense to me. "I don't care, I don't care," she responded to my every threat and objection, and I suddenly thought: "Of course you don't, and why should you? You don't want to be in this place, as long as your life is out there to live, even if that means the street." I thought, then, how much of a loner Linda truly was, as well as a person of the street, who had made so much of her life there. In that light, my protestations could only look as feeble as they actually were, and they ceased.

These things came into sharpest focus when Linda could no longer resist being hospitalized. Every intractable dimension of the human condition was concentrated in the crucible of that room, that floor, that institution. I came to marvel that anyone could get well there—it seemed more likely that if you weren't sick when you went in, you would be before you came out. In saying that, I don't mean to criticize Bellevue Hospital, which as the only resort of treatment for the poor in this area bears the brunt of this epidemic, but whose excellent and dedicated staff makes it the first choice for these same people. I refer instead to the phenomenon of the modern hospital, where vulnerable bodies are at the mercy of every form of harassment and intrusion. Add to that overworked nurses and staff; factors of race and class that could turn an exchange into a delicate undertaking; fear in the presence of death; particular fear in the presence of AIDS; and what I must say I could only interpret in some cases as plain indifference to suffering. No wonder Linda refused treatments and rejected the social pleasantries as she fought against the inevitable.

I came to count it as a blessing that Linda did have the capacity for refusal left to her—so much that was imposed upon her deserved resounding rejection. She was, moreover, possessed of a fineness of spirit—noble, keen, fierce—which it took me, in my presumption and thoughtlessness, a long time to see. It was present in the directness of her gaze once she was no longer able to speak and in her sharp awareness of what was happening around her when it seemed she should be long past that kind of alertness. Stoicism ran very deep in her, accented by a bodily grace (the line of her jaw and throat, the delicate and precise motions of her hands) that the wasting of her body could not destroy. She remembered others and asked for them. She received help in her helplessness with a humility that would put most of us to shame.

Linda had been failing for nearly two weeks when I went up to see her last Friday. Now, her poor frame was gasping for breath, but astonishingly, she met me with her eye when she realized that somebody was there. Alarmed, I left her for a moment to search out a nurse, but quickly changed my mind and came right back. Stroking her hair, I instantly saw that in just the moments of my absence she had changed. I took her hand now as well, and called to her, but with no response. There was time to say, "Linda, it's Meg, and I'm with you," before she closed her eyes and was still.

Linda died as the destitute die, by forces that attack them from within and without. I would like to speak of the presence of God, which is also within and all around us, but that is not mine to say for Linda, who bore the weight of that great suffering. My hope is that she knew the presence of many and of One who loved her, in her last weeks and her final moments.

> "He did not make death and He does not rejoice in the destruction of the living. For He fashioned all things that they might have being . . . For justice is undying." (Wisdom 1:14–15)

Maryhouse, 55 East 3rd Street (1973–present)
Artist: Gary Donatelli

Lena Rizzo

BY JEANNETTE NOEL

The Catholic Worker March-April 1990

ST. PAUL, IN 1 Corinthians 13:12, says, "Now we see darkly as in a distorted mirror, then we shall see very clearly." This quote struck me as I thought about Lena. How we see people clearer once they have gone to their eternal rest. It always amazed me that only good was spoken of those who died. I know now that the scales fall from our eyes and we are able to see Jesus in them.

I love Lena dearly. As I look back on her life, I see a woman who was strong, who stood up to fate. A life which we as a society made difficult for her to survive. Lena was well known on the streets of New York. The *National Geographic Magazine* wrote about her with good taste. Many wrote books about the homeless and used Lena as one of their subjects. Many, in an attempt to bring awareness to their plight, unfortunately ended up taking away what little dignity they had. I saw pictures of Lena in one such book that were degrading, and I was angry and sad to see that the dignity of the poor meant so little to those who wrote about them.

Lena was tough, as one had to be to survive. She was, as we say, "street-wise." For years Lena came to St. Joseph's for food. As was her right (she was an angry woman), she would without warning become violent. This made it impossible for her to live in the house as part of the family. A few years later when Maryhouse was opened, Lena came to stay with us during the winter months, and would return to Fourteenth Street in the spring. She wanted to go back to her turf. Lena would not accept a bedroom but would sleep on a bench outside the auditorium doors in the hallway, her possessions around her where she could keep an eye on them.

During the long winter months, Lena would spend hours sewing. She was creative and I marveled at some of the clothes she made. Every stitch by hand. I am sure that given a chance Lena could have been a dress designer. She was certainly years ahead of her time stylewise. She was also adept with a crochet hook and made many of us hats and scarves of her creation.

The time came, however, when Lena could no longer survive on the streets. She came to stay as part of the family here at Maryhouse. We re-joiced when she agreed to sleep in a bed. Quickly, before she changed her mind, we set one up in the auditorium. I overheard her one day when she answered the phone, telling someone that she had her own room. Lena became a real presence in the house. She spent many hours folding the paper for mailing, she would help serve the evening meal, she shared with others what little she had. As gentle as she had become, she still had a mind of her own and would take no cruel teasing from anyone. She would be quick to make sharp replies to those who would taunt her.

Her greatest joy was the visits from Bernie. He was her pride and joy. She would actually glow when he walked in the door. How she loved him. How she enjoyed his company. Bernie never let her down; he would spend time talking with her, allowing her to experience the dignity that she had been deprived of for so many years. He brought out the best in Lena in a way none of us could.

Around five thirty, after the evening meal, Joan would help Lena go to bed. Never having slept in a bed for many years, her weight made it difficult for her to pull the blankets up to cover her body. Joan had a way of making this a special treat for Lena. When Joan left I inherited this ritual. I look back with shame as I realize how I would make her wait ten or fifteen minutes. How I would become impatient with her, thinking only of my own tiredness, my own discomfort. She would sense my annoyance and look at me with eyes pleading for acceptance, for understanding of her needs. Of course I would melt as she won me over with that look. I would tuck her in, kiss her goodnight, and kid her along a little bit. She would respond with a grateful smile. I would return to my room and ask God's forgiveness for my insensitivity for her needs. I am grateful that I never turned her down.

Lena spent less than a week in the hospital. Many of us went to visit her and tried to encourage her as she lay there with so many of the modern contraptions that helped her breathe. But to her they were frightening. She was diagnosed as having pneumonia. Then after a sonogram they discovered that her lungs were filled with cancer which had spread to the liver. It amazed us how she never complained of pain while here at Maryhouse. I now realize that the only thing Lena wanted from us was love and affection. In my heart I wonder. Did I meet her needs as a child of God? Hopefully I have learned a lesson from my journey over the years with Lena. May she know the fullness of God's love and presence.

BY MICHAEL HARANK

EARLIER ON THE MORNING of the day I received Jeannette's letter telling me of Lena's death, I had noticed on my way to work in downtown Oakland a rather large woman sitting with all her bagged belongings at the entrance to the BART station on Fourteenth Street and Broadway. Somehow, the sight of her flashed me back to an image of Lena camped out near the entrance of the subway on Fourteenth Street at Union Square in New York. This was one of Lena's ports in the area, where she anchored amidst a roaring sea of shoppers, taxi cabs, cheap clothing stores, delis, drug addicts and pushers, business men and women—the flotsam and jetsam of the East Side. These were the people who helped Lena survive on the streets while she camped in the spring, summer, and autumn seasons. She counted on them for a hot cup of coffee or a sandwich, or maybe even a kind word.

Some folks of means spend the harsh New York winters in the tropical breezes of Florida. Not Lena. When the mercury began to fall in the autumn, she would gradually and somewhat reluctantly make her way down to Third Street and Second Avenue to Maryhouse. She knew when it was time to make her trek to Maryhouse and settle into the warm foyer of the main entrance surrounded by her earthly belongings stuffed in bags. These bags would miraculously multiply in the coming months like the loaves and fishes. It was one miracle the Catholic Workers were not pleased with or impressed by.

There, outside the large auditorium adjacent to the offices where she could always sniff out Jennette's presence, and down the hall from the chapel, Lena encamped herself on a long, wooden church bench. There she sewed her quilt-patch clothes, greeted some very surprised guests at the front door, and spun her own political theories of why the atheists ruled the world. The high walls of that foyer entrance hold a multitude of Lena's stories and homilies in the aging cracked plaster.

My most cherished story of Lena was the memorable meeting between her and Mother Teresa. One day Mother Teresa had stopped by the house to pay a visit to Dorothy Day. Accompanied by her friend and biographer, Eileen Egan, Mother had finished her visit with Dorothy and Eileen asked me to take her on a brief "tour" of the house. I gladly agreed. Mother Teresa came out of the chapel after a few minutes of prayer and found herself in the foyer. I began the "tour" with an introduction to Lena, who was lying on her church bench observing all the activity with great scrutiny.

"Mother Teresa, this is Lena. Lena, this is Mother Teresa." Mother reverently clasped her hands together and gently bowed toward Lena—her white sari bending down with a soft movement of reverence. "Pleased to meet you, Lena," she said softly.

Lena looked inquisitively at this unusually attired nun and asked with her characteristic lisp, "Where are ya from?" "Calcutta, India," Mother replied again with a bow. Puzzled, Lena asked, "How did you get here? Did you come on roller skates or toothpicks?" "No," Mother chuckled, flapped her white sari with both elbows, and said, "I flew!" They both laughed. That seemed reasonable to Lena, who was given to some wild flights of imagination.

Impatient with the dragged-out introductory remarks, Lena finally got down to business. Looking Mother directly in the eyes, she said, "Well, now that you are here, do you have a cigarette for me?" It was, as you can imagine, one of Lena's most asked questions to anybody who passed by. Mother Teresa nodded and replied, "I'm sorry, but I do not smoke." Not having any success, Lena went on to the next person with the same, timeworn question. She always found someone around to meet that request.

I hope and pray that St. Peter was ready for Lena's questions when they met in the foyer of the heavenly mansion.

Trinidad Marie

BY TIM LAMBERT

The Catholic Worker March–April 1991

THERE WAS A RAP at the door, and something determined about the woman standing on the other side of it.

It was a day in early spring, a few months after I had moved to Maryhouse. I pretty much knew the ropes, but I did not know this woman. I pushed open the door, and she just looked at me. She was stately. Short, stiff-postured, beautiful coffee-brown skin, properly dressed with a button-down coat and a hat with an ornamented brim—like someone from the deep South, dressed in her Sunday best, with that come-home-from-church authority about her.

I think I said hello. But she just looked at me. Although I knew it was the wrong question, I asked if I could help her. She let loose. I don't remember with what, but words went up and down in a thick accent straight from the Islands. It was easy enough to get the gist—I should step aside.

Just as she reached the head of the stairs, the realization dawned: This must be "Trinidad Marie." I had only heard of her, but never seen her.

She was indeed, as it turned out, coming home from church. That was about the only time you ever stood a chance of seeing her. The rest of the time she kept to her room, leading her own and very private life, never joining us for meals or caring to talk much with us. The church was just around the corner. It was a "storefront" church, with a good-looking brick facade, nicely finished rooms upstairs, and a sign stretching across the front saying "The Universal Church."

I would not have gotten to know her had it not been for her health beginning to fail. I think it was mostly old age. And the less she got out, the

61

faster it set in. We all began to check on her more often, and with a lot of encouragement I too ventured up to her locked door on the third floor. She had a tiny room that had been used as a practice room in this former music school, barely big enough for her bed, a small cupboard, and some clothes hung on the wall. I would knock until she opened. She usually would take a while to respond, often because she had been sleeping, plus she was a little hard of hearing. As she was moving toward the door, I could hear her protestations about why someone was rousing her at this hour. Slowly the doorknob turned, and she would appear in her bedclothes.

Once inside, I would go about my routine. Open up the window for a little fresh air, empty out her wash basin in the hall bathroom and put clean water in it, pick up trash, maybe help her find a piece of clothing or a comb or something dropped on the floor, and empty the "posey." Then we'd eat. I had a few things from downstairs for her, but she also had some tins she kept under her bed. It was almost all sweets, a great variety of them, brought by her pastor. As I'd get her eating, she would insist (and I mean insist) that I had some too.

With her now awake, she would begin enjoying the visit, the chance to talk to someone, get a report on the weather outside, and maybe a little back rub to work out some of the aches. Sometimes she would talk about her past in Trinidad, having a father who was a solicitor, a very loving mother (of thirteen children); and even a bit about her "pre-conversion" days, including some barroom piano playing. "Yes, dearie," she would say. "I could really rattle those keys." She got to like me (not as much as Bernie, for whom she had countless pet names) and I liked her.

As we talked, she always had a lot of advice. Usually it was about finding a good "wifey" for me, and a proper job, since, as good as it was, she didn't think Maryhouse was any place for me to spend my life. Or advice about my family, or just general rules about the way the world works, what to be careful of, and what to be thankful for. After I heard Felton was doing it, I began reading the Bible to her. Afterward she would preach a powerful sermon, or just offer a spontaneous prayer especially for me, asking God to protect me from all my enemies, and bless us both. It was hard to leave. I hate to think how many times I promised, after much prodding, that I would indeed come again before the day was out, knowing full well how crazy things were downstairs, and how unlikely it was I'd see her before another day or two passed.

It all took on greater intensity as she got worse. Many more raps were needed at her door before she would begin to rustle. Over time her eyesight, always poor, went completely. She never went deaf, but I would have to shout. One sad thing was when she got lice, which refused to leave her, despite our following the advice of every major school of thought on how to rid her of them. She long before had forgone her wig, and from underneath appeared gentle white hair that fell a good ways down her back, and which she usually would neatly braid and put up. Eventually it had to be cut short. More often she appeared confused and disoriented, and then the sheets began to be found soiled and wet. Finally, she couldn't move much at all.

It was one of those momentous decisions at Maryhouse, to call the ambulance. Everything inside of me wanted to keep her at home, but we couldn't do it anymore. And our inability to care for her was hastening her downslide. Finally, with her limbs nearly atrophied, and despite her steady resistance, we put in the call.

BY KATHARINE TEMPLE

TRINIDAD MARIE (AND SHE was called that from years back when five or six people named "Mary" or "Marie" lived at Maryhouse) died in the early hours of the day after Christmas. It was well over two years after that day we reluctantly called the ambulance; thirty months of being trundled to the hospital, to a nursing home, and back again.

Pete, who drove the hearse for her burial in Staten Island, told me that the old story about people dying around the holidays is true: they hold on for a time that is important to them. I do not know whether Marie was conscious it was Christmastide, but I do know her Lord was central to her life, and she clung to Him as her faculties had faded one after the other. Because of her strong will, this letting go took a long time.

By the end, she could neither see nor barely hear (though, miraculously, she recognized Bernie and Mark on our very last visit) nor taste, and was usually curled up in a fetal position. And yet, when she sensed a friend by her bed (and it was amazing how the nurses' aides broke our every prejudice about the lack of care in large health institutions), she would say over and over, "It's nice to be nice!" and would recite from long memory, with you, any psalm you might be reading to her.

Eventually she was moved to a hospital we could not reach by public transit, and she died alone—stripped on her death certificate of her name (Martinez having been assumed in the interest of a green card, which was lost before she came to Maryhouse) and so too her origins (listed as "Hispanic" because of the name). It was her hidden soul that went forth to meet her Maker and Savior, sustained, I am sure, by her confidence that "the Lord is my shepherd; I shall not want!"

Katie Campbell

BY JO ROBERTS

The Catholic Worker May 1993

IF YOU CAME ROUND to Maryhouse, Katie would often be the first person you'd meet—sitting out in front of the house, panhandling. She would stay in your mind for her welcome, and for her size—rumored to be over four hundred pounds. On Jennifer's first visit, Katie was sitting on the other side of the door, watching her knock. Eventually, she opened it: "I'm not supposed to open the door, but it's a special occasion: you're here. Are you going to live with us and be a Catholic Worker?" "I guess so." "Good. We need more Catholic Workers." She always pronounced it "Catlick Woiker."

I'd take up her evening pill to her room—"Sit down, why don't you?" I'd sit on the bed, leaning up against her. She'd ask who was helping me with the dishes and floor mopping—"You Catlick Woikers always woik too hard!" And then we'd sit for awhile, and she'd tell me stories.

Katie had been around Maryhouse for a long time. She would often tell me about "Mr. Michael" (Mike Harank) meeting her in Tompkins Square Park, giving her money for a sandwich and telling her to meet him at Maryhouse, where he'd fix up a bed. That was in the late seventies. She had lots of stories: her running away from Manhattan State Psychiatric Hospital, eight months pregnant, and Kassie and Sharon hunting for her all night; then moving to Maryhouse after the birth of her fourteenth child. She told me little about the time before Maryhouse.

Katie was very generous with her friends, very hospitable to strangers. And I've seen her defuse a tense situation by offering someone a cigarette at just the right moment. She'd hold court, sometimes reluctantly, in her room, where people would drop by for a chat and a cigarette; she was always giving out cigarettes. I say reluctantly—Kassie, next door, was often awakened by Katie's yelling when someone in need of a three a.m. smoke woke her a little roughly.

"Spare change, young blood?" often awoke those of us on the front of the house a few hours later; Katie could be out on her pitch as early as a quarter of seven, if she could find someone to open the door. She had a stream of "steady customers." She would always end her request, successful or not, with "I'll pray for you," and I think this spiritual generosity often reaped more earthly rewards.

She did like food. When she homed in on the kitchen table for seconds, people got out of the way. She would sneak back for thirds, if you weren't vigilant, or buy them from a less hungry friend. She'd buy bread and cheese, when she had the money, for a mid-afternoon snack, and would often proffer a bag of chips. Spaghetti was her favorite, from childhood feasts in her Italian family, perhaps. She liked men, too. Particularly Bernie.

Katie had a mouth on her—she was no angel. She knew exactly how to wind people up, which she did gleefully, often for long periods of time. She kept her many friends, nonetheless.

Katie died on February 3, just a few days after her fifty-first birthday. Jennifer and Florence had taken her up to Bellevue with suspected bronchitis in the morning; she'd been feeling so wretched she finally agreed to go. Six painful hours after having been admitted, her heart stopped in the emergency room. Her death was totally unexpected. People in the dining room for supper that night were in a state of shock. "I just can't believe it," Claire kept saying. Then people began to remember her. Pauline and Gloria and I were agreeing that now, in heaven, Katie would be given all the seconds she could want. A few days later she was cremated by her family.

I have a picture up in my room—Katie on her chair on the doorstep, me standing beside her. It is hard to realize that she's gone. When I'm in the dining room I think she's upstairs, when I'm in my room I think she's in the dining room. We thank God for her life with us—she was a great person to share a house with. We all miss her very much.

Preston Colby Lewis
Artist: Tony Gawron

Preston Colby Lewis

BY JANE SAMMON

The Catholic Worker August–September 1995

WAKING UP EARLY ONE morning, scheduled to take the house, my mind turned to Preston Lewis. As I groped round for something to don, it was the thought of pockets—those practical holders for pen, medicine, envelopes, keys—which led to memories of Preston and his strict criterion for keeping an everyday shirt that might make its way to the clothing room.

"Does it have pockets, Janey?" he would query, squinting at an item I thought would look spiffy on his long, lean frame. All well and good, but if it didn't pass muster in the pockets department, the disappointment was obvious, a *harrumph* and a little shake of his large head included.

"It's all right, I'll just wait for something else to come in. Thanks anyway." Strangely enough, it was at these moments of shirt shopping with Preston when I might recall the dictum of Peter Maurin, about having a functional rather than an acquisitive society. How would the founder of the Catholic Worker movement view clothing which was more decorative than functional? Yes, I just bet Peter would concur with Mr. Lewis; a shirt without pockets is like a book without words.

Ah, but don't get me wrong. Preston could dress up. Could he ever! At weddings, May Day celebrations, Thanksgiving, Christmas—he was a wonder in a three-piece suit—worn only on such special occasions. All I can say is that the men of our community would admire his style, and the ladies would murmur their approval when Preston Lewis took his first stroll down to the kitchen on festive days, searching for that first cup of coffee.

When I came to the Catholic Worker in the early seventies, Preston was not around, though I heard his name every once in a while, for he had lived at St. Joseph House in the late sixties. Preston arrived again one night a few years later, a tall, thin man with glasses framing an angular face, large ears, a prominent nose—a handsome countenance set off with a goodly amount of loosely curling gray hair. I cannot readily bring to mind the sequence of events after that, but in he came, occupying in time the room which he shared with Mr. Wong on the third floor.

We can never adequately describe the dead; panegyrics of any sort do not reveal the complex creatures that most of us are. I know that Preston had, in his younger years, something of the wanderlust in him. Perhaps it was attributable to his having to move in his infancy from Boothbay Harbor, Maine, down to Massachusetts, to live with relatives after both of his parents died in the great flu epidemic of 1918. At what age did he take to the road again? I couldn't say, but his travels within the U.S. seemed extensive, a good period of time being spent in California. He mentioned working at some of those places most familiar to men of few economic means—the Salvation Army, Goodwill, this mission on Skid Row, that flophouse. Preston cleaned, cooked, I think he even did a stint as an unarmed security guard in one of those establishments, and, yes, he sorted things in their clothing rooms.

It is quite possible that, had the opportunity arisen, Preston might have gone to university. He loved to read, he loved to learn, a man with an insatiable appetite for the study of history, particularly the Civil War era. The life of Lincoln riveted his attention, and I sometimes wonder if it was perhaps due to a certain physical similarity to the tall, gaunt president.

This love of learning was enriched by a tremendous use of and support for the New York Public Library system. He made friends among librarians, financially contributed from his small pension check, and borrowed books with great regularity. Many times we would run into Preston on the street, his books clasped to his side. "I'm going to the library, probably the one over on Sixth Avenue this time." He did not confine library visits to the one closest to our houses and he eventually became friendly with the women of the Hamilton Fish Park Library, a good walk from us over by the FDR Drive. Of course he bought a few books himself, but the rule was the library circulation for a good read. As his life in the house went on, as he got weaker from the cancer which was first diagnosed almost three years ago, several of us took turns at getting those books back before or at least right on their due date.

Preston appreciated music, particularly of a classical style. Now, even though his book habits were circulatory, his record collection was bought off the street, or in secondhand shops throughout the neighborhood. He loved opera, Puccini, Verdi, Strauss. He had a wonderful recording of Rubinstein playing Chopin and was glad to share the wealth with one who had similar musical proclivities. Then of course, there was baseball, a devotion which lasted even after the infamous strike of 1994. Not to say that Preston didn't offer his view on the great American pastime that became an industry, but he had too much faith in the goodness of athletic competition to let it keep him down. He did buy a couple of baseball books, one being an encyclopedia of sport.

As I said before, panegyrics are no substitute for keen description, including insights into those little faults which make us human. Let us be honest: Preston Lewis was not the sort of person who cheerfully accepted an empty coffee pot. Catholic Workers who have passed through the New York house, who lived with this man, could attest to that. If you are ever up near Boston, ask Robbie Gamble what an empty coffee pot meant to Mr. Lewis. Not that he got angry, the fit of pique was a bit more subtle, yet rather palpable to those who knew him. He would slowly amble over to the area of the kitchen where the pot sat. Then came the moment of truth: the clear glass container told the bitter tale—the last drop had been drained. Preston would issue a quick and audible sigh, sometimes accompanied by that all-purpose word of annoyance, "Dammit!" That was it, maybe a few more facial contortions to indicate his disgust, but then the quick recovery. "Well, I guess I should have just gotten down here a bit earlier, oh well." The man was also a great milk drinker, a worthy complement to the little Table Top or Betty Jane fruit pies that he kept in supply up on his bedroom windowsill. Not to mention his vanilla wafers or, really, any sort of cookie would do—they were among his gastronomical delights. Oh, the pain of a non-meat night at the house for Preston! Joe McKenzie-Hamilton summed it up well: "Preston never met a vegetable he liked," preferring, any old day, a prepackaged hot dog—bun not necessary. Menthol cigarettes were another weakness and it is easy to think that cancer was abetted by this habit.

Now, the reader might ask if Preston did any sort of work during his years at the Catholic Worker. If you're a longtime subscriber, the chances are good that Preston labeled your paper at one time or another, for this was his greatest contribution to the mailing of *The Catholic Worker*. He got to be a whiz at remembering zip codes of little-known regions of the country. "Aliquippa, PA? 15001. Beebe Plain, VT? 05823." In fact, we used to tease him about going on a quiz show called "Zip Code."

Our homage to the dead helps us to remember their beings, to bring them back to life in another form. I remember some of the things surrounding those last few weeks of Preston's life; I'm sure that others remember much more. The close friendship which Preston shared with Lynn was deep, considerate, and moving; she did much to assure his comfort when he last entered the hospital. Others of us came and went, doing our best to keep him, as well as ourselves, aware of our links in the Catholic Worker movement, as family one to another. Dan, Sabra, Lynn, Michelle, and I got there for a surprise birthday party a mere two and a half weeks before his death. We hid in the hospital hall, lit candles on the cake we brought along and sang our way into his room. The baseball game was on his small bedside TV, but our presence seemed well received despite the interruption. Lynn made his card quite creative and well drawn with a photo of Dolly Parton, country western singer, a little joke between the two of them. On that day, there was nothing too obvious to indicate his quick entry the next day into the ICU, breathing difficulties and the possibility of a slight stroke sending him there.

Then, his waking times decreased, his leaving of us took the form of a semi-coma, an inability to talk with us anymore. But we kept our hearts full of hope for his recovery and prayed he might come back to his home on the third floor. In the ICU, we did our best to keep talking with him, despite his growing unconsciousness. We would stare helplessly at the large, noble-looking elder lying prone in the bed, and, in time, resolute, nearing the end of his days. This was the time when the holding of his hand, the playing of his kind of music on the hospital room's radio were the only things we seemed able to do. We know that, at a dying person's bedside, the mind leaps back to other scenes, as we observe the still form which once knew laughter, strength, and language. How many times, back home, had this man, growing thinner and more frail, been lifted up from the floor by Carmen in the middle of the night, after a bout of weakness, a loud thud, a cry for help? And now this. Yet we kept our watch as best we could, spelling each other at the hospital, sometimes coming up in parts, to stand and wait and pray . . . Brian Harte and I walked down from the printers one day, expecting that it would soon be over. For Brian, on his way to his sister's wedding, it was a moment of farewell to a fellow third-floor resident.

On a beauteous Saturday, June 17, Siobhan stopped at the hospital. She arrived around noon and stayed till almost one. She sensed something imminent in Preston's life that day, concluding that he was soon to die. About an hour and half later, Sabra and I got calls from St. Vincent's with the news of Preston's passing. The young doctor at the other end of the phone seemed awkward. "Did anyone plan on coming over here when he's, ah, still in the room?" he wondered. I said yes, hung up and called Sabra over at St. Joe's to see if she would like to go. At first it didn't look like it would work since she was taking the house, but once again, the communal response was tremendous. Tony, Eric, and others took care of First Street; Sabra got ahold of Marion and the three of us went there to say our last goodbyes. We buried Preston at Silver Mount Cemetery on Staten Island. I'll always remember how beautiful Barbara Jackson looked in her dressy skirt and blouse. I can still hear Lynn's voice reading from Preston's own copy of the Hebrew Scriptures, "To everything, there is a season . . ."

We called as many people as we could think of for a memorial service the following week. I think Preston would have enjoyed it. An astoundingly large crowd gathered for reflections after Father Anthony's Mass. Nurses, librarians, former Catholic Workers like Jim Kelly and his wife Lisa and baby Liam. Sam Turner, with his wife Liisa and their little guy, Eliot, all came to offer their memories. Lynn and Dan read from Scripture. Bill Antalics recited a passage from Carl Sandburg's biography of Lincoln. Joe offered some words from one of Preston's favorite baseball books. The library friends moved the gathering with testimonies for a staunch supporter of the library system. Sabra arranged the room in her usual beautiful way and Siobhan found one of those little fruit pies, but baked her famous brownies, too. You could almost feel the presence of a tall, gangly man slowly moving through the kitchen. And on that particular night, Preston Lewis, you'll be happy to know that the coffee pot was full. Rest in peace!

James Taylor

BY JOE MCKENZIE-HAMILTON

The Catholic Worker December 1995

JAMES "BIRD" TAYLOR DIED sometime this September, somewhere in the city. I had the good fortune of knowing him for four years before his recent, rather sudden death. He deserves a lot more than these few short words, as he deserved a lot better in life.

Bird was a regular on the soup line, a tall, thin, bearded black man in his early forties. He was always easy to spot in his trademark porkpie hat and vest. His vest was a classic, festooned as it was with a creative assortment of the most interesting buttons Bird would find and sew on, until the finished vest looked like the jeweled scales of a dragon. I wonder if this vest wasn't also some kind of symbolic armor for him, keeping the constant thrust and parry of street life in check. Perhaps that's what helped him keep on keeping on, and doing so with such grace, humor, and good will.

Bird would usually come up the block pushing a wagon full of the odds and ends he'd find and peddle on the streets, when the cops would let him. In recent days, that was less and less often. The cafés and restaurants that have sprung up here on the Lower East Side (the vanguards of gentrification) have made the sidewalks, where folks like Bird had worked for years, contested ground. The sidewalk cafés covet the space for their expanding tables and "outdoor ambience" and have, in the words of one peddler, "the loot to give us the boot." And so, moved along, locked up, pushed out, getting by for folks like Bird becomes an even more complicated and precarious affair.

Bird saw the cruelty and crassness of it all. As he'd unfold his lawnchair or stretch out on top of his cart outside during the soup line, he'd hold court. He had a sharp, wry humor that gloried in teasing out the contradictions and the ridiculousness of the situation of the Lower East Side. For example, it amused him to no end that the whole push against the homeless and homeless peddlers was being conducted by the city under the banner of the Quality of Life Task Force. He could really get ripping on that one! My conversations with Bird were always a bright spot in a day. Like sun on stained glass, he brought out the best of the situation. Our conversations were as easy and expansive as his voice, rambling along contentedly from one thing to another, from the sad fate of the Knicks or Yankees to different Biblical verses Bird had memorized.

Bird was a pleasure to be around, a serious man who knew just how not to take things too seriously. He got his nickname for his love of birds and had been a bird handler at some time in his life. I remember once watching him as he deftly, and with considerable patience, removed a wire that had gotten tangled up in a pigeon's feet. The moment summed up the man: compassionate, considerate, and kind.

I was knocked breathless when this once-vibrant man came to the door of St. Joseph House this last September after an absence of many weeks. He was rail thin, shallow breath rattling in his chest, and his face carved to the bone. He had lost so much weight and was weak and exhausted. At first, I honestly didn't recognize that ravaged, ruined man as my friend. I don't know how long AIDS had hovered in his life, but now it had swooped down with a terrible vengeance. Bird had been in a public hospital in Brooklyn, but had gotten lost jumping through bureaucratic hoops and was discharged to the streets. Although he was obviously deathly sick, he didn't receive the necessary M11Q form from the hospital to prove his AIDS virus. This prevented him from getting the treatment he needed. Even those places offering the intensive and specialized care that he required, which wanted to help him, could do nothing without that form.

Through God's grace and a ton of phone calls, we found a place that would help him get the medical care he needed. Bird promised to call me to let me know when he would be placed. I never heard a word, until news came that he had died. His living was hard enough; I hope his dying was peaceful. May he rest in peace and may his memory inspire us to keep on keeping on in the work of justice and compassion with the same humor and tenacity he always demonstrated.

Thomas Masciotta

BY CARMEN TROTTA

The Catholic Worker December 1996

THOMAS MASCIOTTA DIED IN the bed he had occupied for some nine years here at St. Joseph House. The death occurred in the wee hours of the morning, and so the house arose to the unexpected, unwanted new fact: Death's intrusion, a permanent imposition on our lives.

It was twelve hours before the medical examiner could come to "confirm the death." These hours would serve for the poor man's only wake. Hence, a few of us kept a dutiful bedside vigil. Most of those who live here, others from Maryhouse, and a handful of neighbors came to pay their respects, to view for the last time this brother, friend, and (let it be said) in a few instances, nemesis. Each encounter represented a relationship terminated abruptly. Each would conjure memories of its living self among the mourners—simultaneously warming and rending the heart. "Blessed are those who mourn."

Although Tommy's death at fifty-two was unexpected, given his health and habits it could not be deemed shocking. It was, however, surprisingly peaceful, a great mercy. For now, given his placid corpse, we can more easily imagine him amidst the ease and wholeness which had utterly eluded him for the past four years—a time during which he fought an increasingly fierce battle with the literal disintegration of his personality: insanity. For in addition to being an epileptic, an alcoholic, and a chain smoker afflicted with emphysema, Tommy lived with schizophrenia. For many years, Tommy suffered auditory hallucinations—menacing voices calling to him from within his own head. Over the years, these increased in volume and frequency.

75

Doctors proposed a variety of medicines in various dosages and configurations. At times, a queasy stability was achieved. Tommy sought further stability in the use of alcohol, a ruse that began to backfire in his last years. Tommy's paranoia would flare up. He might come into the kitchen having had a few, sit and glower away in the corner. Dour, his eyes lit with unwarranted anger and accusation. Spurious arguments were provoked full of verbal abuse.

How to respond? Sometimes we would just endure Tommy's hell. He would sleep it off, come downstairs in the morning, variously evasive or contrite. Other times, the abuse was too much and he was asked to leave the house for the night. At this, he might throw down the gauntlet. He was finished with us, he was never coming back. He'd demand all his belongings. We would give him his coat and tell him we would talk further in the morning. He'd threaten to call the police; we'd tell him he should probably sober up first. He'd slam the door on his way out.

In retrospect alone, what follows is nearly comic. Tommy had nowhere to go. For as long as Tommy lived with us, he never ventured more than five blocks away unaccompanied. Like other of his habits, I did not realize their relationship to his affliction until the very end. He could not leave the block in his last year because of the voices. He was too afraid. So, he'd leave us forever and go sit across the street!

The next morning you might open the door to see him on the stoop, defiant next to a 16 oz. can in a paper bag. Various people would go over to try to talk with him during the day. He'd be argumentative or dismissive or both. It was a standoff that could last for a week.

At times, the issue raised itself. "Perhaps we just can't have him back. We need to wash our hands of him." The allusion is deliberate; we did no such thing. Eventually, he would return, absolutely exhausted. A few days would be spent in a detox, convalescing. Typically, he had little recollection of the past days. Warily, he would make apologies. Warily, he was welcomed back.

In retrospect, that is, free of the raw demoralization that accompanied these scenes, I find myself almost nostalgic and thankful for them. Simply, he had broadened my life experience and I cannot now narrate these scenes without a sort of rueful smile. Indeed, I dwell unduly upon them. More, all were alcohol induced. For, outside of these episodes, Tommy never lost the basic integrity of his person. He never "went insane."

Just a week before he died, I visited him in the hospital. The voices had grown increasingly insidious. First, they infiltrated his dreams. Then, a woman's voice joined the chorus. Finally, and most frighteningly, the voices were no longer "in his ear." They came from outside the door, behind him—anywhere. It became almost impossible for him to distinguish real voices from the curses and threats his mind was generating. Tommy began to fear that his mind's reflexive answers would become audible, that he would speak to them out loud. To him, this was the ultimate indignity. I came in with a cup of coffee for him, but he was not to be bothered; it would go cold in my hand. He was sitting up and seemed to be listening intently. I heard some murmuring and noticed his lips moving. I thought the worst had come to pass.

I called to him, "Tommy, who are you talking to?" "I'm not talking," he explained. "I'm singing. If I can remember the words to old songs, I don't concentrate on the voices." My God, what a pitched and silent battle. No, by sheer will he never "went insane." A hard-won victory, I would insist. Fate could not break him, it would have to take him whole. And did. A Pyrrhic victory perhaps, but the crucifixion might be similarly regarded; beautiful for its very futility. Ironically, in death as in life, sanity was Tommy's gift. His widespread eyes regarded the larger world with a jaded resignation. Nothing much out there ever tallied. Happiness would be found in a smaller circle: friends, family, a modicum of comfort and security.

His own experience was a sobering/lethal mix of poverty, ill fortune, betrayal, and tragedy. Its details need to remain in confidence. The broad outlines will be quite enough. Born in New York City in 1944, his childhood was marred by the prolonged absence of his father. The mother of six, whom Tommy adored, could not support the children. Tommy's early years were spent in a Catholic orphanage on Staten Island.

The reassembled family to which the adolescent Tommy returned proved to be a temporary arrangement, and he was rushed into adulthood, becoming the breadwinner and caring for younger siblings. He received some vocational training and took up a variety of jobs—making machine parts at a tool and die factory, waxing floors for the Veterans Administration. These were his best years, over a decade. He took pride in having assumed his responsibilities. He was a working man. The remaining siblings moved on and out. Tommy would care for his mother.

Then came a decade of improbable, mounting ill fortune. The voices began. Stays in psychiatric institutions made his work life sporadic. Next came the epileptic seizures. Given his overall medical conditions, Tommy was deemed disabled and began picking up a check. There would, however, be enough work right at home—Tommy's mother was diagnosed with cancer. He would care for her until the bitter end. He paid for her burial plot in a Catholic cemetery, along with a second beside it for himself. He would never occupy that grave; he gave it instead to one of the three siblings who would be murdered in separate incidents in the intervening years.

After his mother's death, Tommy began drinking heavily. Not to the point of sloppiness, but sedation. Still, bereft as he was, Tommy allowed some old friends who'd been evicted from their apartment to move in with him. They began using drugs in his apartment and stealing from him. Tommy took his next check and just left, out to the street to join the swollen ranks of New York's homeless.

He lived out on the streets for over a year. Somehow, he was remarkably free of bitterness or self-pity. He was not, however, responsible enough to keep up with his medical needs. The seizures occasionally left him a bloody mess. This is when folks from the Catholic Worker met him. The idea was to stabilize him on his medications and see what he wanted to do from there. Shortly, it became clear that he wanted nothing more than what he now had with us. He flowered. He was a helpful, indeed an affable sort, so he stayed.

He became our ambassador on the block. He enjoyed the sun on the neighbor's stoops, his coffee, surreptitious beer, and cigarettes. He'd wave a smiling "good day" to any face that became familiar. People enjoyed it, and responded in kind. Acquaintances developed. He'd tell people how nice it was to live in the "Catlick Workers." I think he needed the assurances of friendly, known faces—security. He enjoyed good conversation, too, and could be insightful and bluntly honest within the narrow confines of his own experience.

Most of his best friends were women. Annie, Barbara, Berta, Bettina, Dana, Sincere, Thora, Vincenza, with each of these he maintained gentle, longterm relations. They took time together in parks and diners, even a few excursions out in the country. When away, the women would send him post cards, which truly delighted him. Indeed, these, along with a single old photograph of his mother, were among the few possessions he left behind. Oh, Tommy! The demands of your happiness were so simple!

A scene comes to mind: Vincenza working away in the kitchen. She's a lively sort, every bit as Italian as Tommy and a few inches shorter.

Tommy would be relaxing with a cigarette, arms folded on the table, his head perched upon them. He'd watch in bemused admiration as "Vinny" worked with all the quick energy of a hummingbird. The energy was infectious. Tommy would call out in humorous encouragement: "Go get 'em, Vinny Barbarino!" The phrase never failed to get a smile.

He was also toothless. He tried dentures once but found them troublesome. He had but the slightest concern for his appearance. Plus, this toothlessness did not keep him from his favorite treats: sausage-and-pepper heroes and pizza. He'd just joyously maul them with his gums. I found this so comical; when he would chew, his handsome, rugged face would sort of collapse. He'd laugh along as he swallowed, then smack his lips and warn me: "Take care of your teeth, Carmen, or you'll end up like this."

The day we buried Tommy was not without its poetic moments. First, it rained. Tommy loved the rain, absolutely nothing soothed him so. As long as the rain fell, he would sit by the window and listen to it. If it rained at night, he'd pull a blanket out on the fire escape and sleep there.

Then Mattie, our neighbor and a loyal friend who shared countless days on First Street with Tommy, built a full-sized church altar for him and placed it in the no-parking zone in front of the house. It was complete with cloth and candles, icons, flowers, and a central crucifix. Within hours, the police pulled up to this curiosity. They looked it over, asked a few questions, and, bless them, let it stand for three days. Anonymously, someone placed a Mass card on it. It was signed, "A friend of Dorothy's."

At the cemetery that raw day, the orange earth opened its maw to receive the casket. Kassie chose the Scripture readings. First, Jeremiah's terrible lamentation: "He has walled me about so that I cannot escape . . . Though I call and cry for help, He shuts out my prayer. He has blocked my way with hewn stone. He has made my paths crooked." (Lamentations 3:1–9)

Then, from John, the words of Mary and Martha. The words that brought the sting of tears to the eyes of Christ Himself, somehow anticipating His most astounding miracle. "Lord, if You had been there, my brother would not have died." Indignant, they knew that death's contradiction should not and could not be the final word. "I am the Resurrection and the Life . . . Do you believe?" (John 11:17–27)

In a semicircle we sang a song. Suddenly, Mattie broke from the line, ripped off his jacket, ran and placed it on the casket. He came back, shaking with indignant grief, explaining, "So he wouldn't be cold. I don't want him to be cold."

That night, we had Mass in the kitchen. Father Bill Brisotti began by reminding us of the presence of God in our midst and of the presence of Tommy. We took a lengthy silence. Then, he opened things up; people maybe needed to talk. Tommy had left us so quickly, there was much yet unresolved. Offerings were made: pieties, affectionate vignettes. Tommy's generosity was remembered. In that pleasant context, other offerings could be made: the consternation Tommy had caused. It all stewed around for over an hour. Then it melted, I think, into remorse.

Gathered around Tommy on that final day was a struggling faith community, transfigured by humility. It was the community that Tommy had so lacked for his entire life. By faith we could face our shortcomings, our inattention. God may yet count our faith as righteousness. Thus, by faith alone we will be saved.

To conjure pleasant memories of Tommy is easy. But this writing has forced me to contemplate again his great suffering, a topic the mind prefers to avoid. Scripture, too, calls us to contemplate suffering. There is a story which Christ says must be told whenever the Gospel is preached. It is the story of Mary of Bethany, the contemplative who foresaw Christ's crucifixion and recognized it as more than another beautiful, futile gesture (John 12:1–8). In her prayers, Mary had distilled all the suffering of the poor into a fragrant, pure nard, or "faith" nard, which she then poured over the feet of Christ. Some condemned her for this foolish extravagance, but Christ commended her. For He would raise this nard up with Him on the Cross, above the seeming futility of its extraction and distillation in time and, by His love, transform it into the active agent of our salvation.

Your suffering, too, Tommy, has been lifted up and called beautiful.

Bobby West, #731

1964–1997

BY KATHARINE TEMPLE

The Catholic Worker October–November 1997

Dear Katharine Temple,

Our friend Bobby West was executed on July 29, 1997, by a lethal injection. I hope there will be an obituary in *The Catholic Worker*. He was a vital spokesperson for the voiceless thousands on U.S. Death Rows. I first read his words in the *CW*.

In Christ the Revolutionary,

Gretchen Laugier

I, TOO, MET BOBBY through his first contribution to the paper, "A View of Civilization from Death Row in Texas," which began:

> The death penalty. Every man, woman, and idiot has been pro-nouncing and spelling this thing wrong. I'm not the son of Webster, but I think I can help. It's spelled r-e-v-e-n-g-e. (*CW*, October–November 1987)

At the time, at age twenty-three, he had already been on death row in Huntsville for four years, and he was to remain there for about another decade. But he did not remain in silence. He wrote constantly, and there is no doubt in my mind that he would want this writing to be his memorial.

Although he pursued his own case, his particular fate was not his focal point. He did not write, for instance, to protest his own innocence, nor to claim mistaken identity, nor to announce a personal conversion to nonviolence in jail. Rather, his passion was to raise consciousness about the reality of capital punishment, in order to bring about its abolition.

> My reason for writing is to deal in fact and let you know the truths that the system isn't going to tell you because, if they did, then you would know that the criminals and prisoners are not the whole problem. We are just the students of the problem, the system's off-spring. So, in the middle of all these lies and hate, what should we do? . . . It's time that people came together in the name of truth, instead of yelling "Kill them!" and "Punish them!" in the name of revenge, and calling it justice to cover the lies. Keep one thing in mind while you pretend it doesn't matter: I am reaching out by writing, instead of reacting through violence. I also believe in the cliché, "What goes around comes around," which means your reaction to this dictates what will eventually come around to you. Why do things have to keep getting worse and worse? When will you realize that punishment by control, correction by fear, does not work, and the only alternative left is compassion, humanity, and concern for the betterment of people? We must move forward because we are already too far behind.
>
> It's long past time we realize that the present system is broken, and, in order to keep from getting hurt over and over again, we must become meliorators and fix it. Until that's done, what goes around will keep coming around, for the system, to us, to you.
>
> James Baldwin wrote: "The moment we cease to hold each other / The moment we break faith with one another / The sea engulfs us and the light goes out."
>
> No wonder it's been so dark in here. (CW, June–July 1989)

Bobby wrote to the end, not only for this paper but also in *Endeavor, Live Voices from Death Row* (a newspaper that Bobby helped to start and edit), his own "Newsbriefs" (a summary of executions around the country and developments, state by state, in capital punishment legislation), a voluminous correspondence, and, finally, a thirty-day diary he left with his lawyer. His campaign was not simply the theoretical and statistical exposé, so much as a portrayal of the realities on death row. Another example:

> Insanity is a threatening thing in here, because nearly everybody is living on the brink of it, the system feeds it to us, and we don't want anything to do with it. Being forced to live in violent surroundings

teaches a man to attack first and not wait to be attacked. With that in mind, when insanity comes in the form of a person, the outcome is a matter of mechanics, the attack is inevitable.

What we have here is a confused, twisted shell of a man that is being psychologically and physically attacked from all sides. A man that has lost contact with reality and is being punished for something he cannot control . . . What is the problem with getting proper psychological attention for the insane on Death Row? Are we afraid to put any more money into capital punishment . . . or are we so blood-thirsty we enjoy seeing them suffer? "The degree of civilization in a society can be judged by entering its prisons" (Dostoevsky, *The House of the Dead*). (*CW*, October–November 1987)

Above all, Bobby, in his fierce angers and loyalties, was able to translate onto paper people on death row from being lifeless statistics to being persons of flesh and blood. This gift was never clearer than in the last piece he wrote for the paper, an obituary for his friend Dusty:

By the courts and the people of Texas, he was condemned to die. By the system, he was housed for a decade plus, in the cell beside me. A decade is a long time, and on 11–22–94 they decided it was enough, enough time, enough life. And now, with you, I share all that's left besides the memories, the long, long silence that comes from what was, what always will be, my friend. (*CW*, January–February 1995)

As the time for Bobby's own execution approached, he continued to write, mainly letters. His last one to me, of the fifteenth of July, was quintessential Bobby West. At the top, as part of the date was "Day 5438," a reminder of his exact time on death row, and he ended with:

I was expecting a stay, wasn't very concerned about none of the things they were saying, but now it's all modified, urgency in the things I want to do, and, while I am doing one thing, like writing this letter, I am thinking about the next things I have to do. Right now, the days are blending into each other, moving a bit too fast. I quit recreating in order to have those extra 2 hours to write, but they don't seem to be doing any good. Oh yeah, they cut the recreation down from 3 hours to 2. Their next move is to reclassify everybody down here. There will be 3 levels of status, the first being no different from what's happening now, the 2nd and 3rd will take everything away from people: radios, typewriters, fans, commissary privileges. Yep, things can indeed always get worse than they are.

I'm sending your picture back with this, no need to leave it laying around in here. If a miracle happens, I will want it back, but, for now, I want to keep it safe.

I'm going to have to keep this one short, so I can try to send as many notes out of here as possible, thanking all of the people who have written and helped. I do, as always, hope that this reaches you and finds you in the very best of health and spirits, and knowing that you are in my thoughts and I'm wishing you a world full of peace and love.

Lots of Peace and Hope,

Bobby

Carmen Hernandez

BY SABRA MCKENZIE-HAMILTON

The Catholic Worker August–September 1998

FOR THE THREE NOVEMBERS I knew Carmen Hernandez, I always forgot her birthday. It was November 8, the same as Dorothy Day's, which ought to have made it more obvious. In retrospect, I realize how fitting it was that "Carmelita," as we called her, never mentioned it, and would sit reverently at Dorothy's Memorial Mass, remembering another instead. She was one of the most dignified women I have ever met.

She came to St. Joe's in 1995, and lived on the fourth floor for over two years. About a year and a half earlier, she had come alone to New York from Puerto Rico with the hopes of starting a new life. She lived with her sister and her sister's family on the Lower East Side for a short while, and left because of some irreconcilable differences. She then found an apartment with a woman she met from church. Carmelita's roommate suddenly had to leave or lost the lease, and she had to find yet another place to live. Unfortunately, the small welfare money she earned cleaning city office buildings could not sustain her, and she was forced to look into the women's shelter system. She was petrified.

I remember receiving the call from a kind woman at our local Church of the Most Holy Redeemer. She told me about Carmelita's situation, that she was on the waiting list for public housing. I had never worked directly with the public housing system in New York City, but I knew that the wait could be very long. She had already been waiting nearly two years. Providentially, however, there was a bed available on the women's floor at St. Joe's, and the community was willing to provide her with temporary hospitality until we could figure out what was happening with her housing status.

That's when the magic took place. Carmen was a marvelous presence and a delightful companion. She spoke very little English, but was able to communicate with most everyone. She was extremely faithful, always attending the Tuesday Masses at St. Joe's and involved with various groups at Our Lady of Sorrows Church. At times, she seemed timid and overwhelmed by this house of mostly men, with soup line madness and crowded rooms. At others, she was jovial and open, losing a bit of that hardened reserve she had cultivated over the last four decades of her life. We knew she had been married and divorced, but were all surprised to learn that she was a grandmother, and she giggled when she told us the secret. She was very beautiful and looked years younger than her age.

I continued to help Carmelita follow up on the waiting lists, calling monthly and realizing how difficult it was to find anyone who could give me new information other than, "We'll let her know when something is available." And, although the community told Carmelita that she could remain at St. Joe's until something came up, she never felt entitled to her bed, and later her room, living always with a sense of precarity and insecurity.

In August of 1996, Carmelita called me and asked if I could come over to visit her. (I was living in an apartment across the street.) She seemed reluctant to ask me to come by, since I had given birth a few weeks earlier, but she really needed to talk. I could tell something had happened, and, when I arrived, she was in tears, with a picture of the Blessed Mother in her hands. She told me that the doctors had found a lump on her right breast that they thought was cancer. She told me that, in Puerto Rico some years before, she had a melanoma removed on her left arm, along with the adjacent lymph nodes. The precarity in her life was increasing.

Over the next two years, some of Carmelita's story unfolded in appointments and waiting rooms across the city—housing, public assistance, disability assessments, hospitals, chemotherapy, oncologists, surgeons, cancer support services, realtors, and emergency rooms. Before she was approved for a Section 8 apartment in the fall of 1997, the cancer had spread to her left breast. After we survived the demoralizing experience of locating a decent apartment approved by the dying federal housing service, the cancer was in her lungs.

The other part of her story must be told in the language of faith. I came to understand Carmelita's journey as a kind of long loneliness from which she collected amazing strength and, ultimately, learned how to reach out to others, including her family. She had been such a seriously private person that she wanted very few people to know about her illness and suffering. In fact, rather than let fellow parishioners know she was undergoing intense chemotherapy, she bore their ridicule instead, when a few acquaintances made fun of her "new hair style," even tugging at her wig to see if it was real or not. It was only when her mother, son, and daughter from Puerto Rico, and her oldest daughter from California came together to visit with her at Christmas, that she began to tell others about how sick she really was. She received visitors from church for the first time when she went into the hospital for pneumonia over the holidays. It was then that she also reconciled with her sister, who became her most consistent local support. And so it went.

Although Carmelita's insurance, Center Care, one of the new private affiliates with Medicaid, surprisingly provided her with an excellent and kind oncologist, they were reluctant to offer frequent home care in the ensuing months. She needed this help, especially after her debilitating chemotherapy every three weeks. Fortunately, her mother returned from Puerto Rico in late April to spend a few spring months with her (she had gotten quite ill herself from the winter cold in December). At this point, however, Carmelita was only able to sustain the chemo while in the hospital. Also, the cancer had spread to her spine.

I was out of town for two weeks in May. When I returned, I called her apartment, then the hospital, then her sister. No one was home. I finally reached her daughter in California, who had just returned from Puerto Rico that day. Carmelita had died at Beth Israel Hospital in New York City on Saturday, May 16. Her family had taken her to San Sebastián for burial that week. She was forty-eight years old, and is survived by a loving family which includes nine grandchildren.

I am a privileged person because I knew Carmen Hernandez. I believe our community at the Catholic Worker is privileged as well. For it was there that she first began to open up a bit about her life, her illness, and her needs. The women on the fourth floor were especially good to her over the years, and I know she considered all of them her friends.

Carmelita's daughter told me that over three hundred people came to her funeral in Puerto Rico. I hope she saw that she was never, at any given point, really alone.

Our Sister Jeanette Chin

BY TANYA THERIAULT

The Catholic Worker August–September 2001

ONE OF THE SOURCES of wisdom residing within the walls of Maryhouse and one of my most witty guides as to the ins and outs of this place is Sister Jeanette. Sister Jeanette has eased my mad mind on several occasions with timely and important lines, such as "We're all a little crazy." And she would know, since Sister has lived at Maryhouse for over ten years and was a long-time friend of the Catholic Worker before that. Sister Jeanette, in her time spent here, has developed a unique and true sense of community. An understanding and appreciation for one another's insanity? Most definitely.

Of all that could be said about Sister, I will say this—she has, during recent trying and frightening times, let me be with her. We've been going to a nearby clinic a lot lately. Days filled with multiple lab tests, doctor's appointments, poking and prodding, are exhausting for me, and no one is even touching me. I imagine that the anxiety of going to the appointments, in addition to the physical demands of actually getting to the clinic are, at this point, more burdensome than what ails Sister. However, few people who cross our path throughout the day of a clinic visit would know this. From the ambulette driver to the guards at the security desk of the clinic, to the nurses, Sister continually spreads about her kind and rugged spirit. Whether she throws up a wave, yells "I love ya!" in her gravelly voice or giggles at the cuteness of a child, Sister Jeanette is known at the clinic to be generous with her well wishes . . .

The biggest concern of the people I come across during our day there is the nature of the relationship between Sister Jeanette and myself. I have been asked if I am Sister's social worker, her home health care attendant, or

88

her granddaughter. I have even been accused of being in the Peace Corps. (I kid you not. Those words were used.) The response, "We're friends," or "We live together," just doesn't seem to be enough for these inquiring minds. But they are the ones left unfulfilled by this friendship, as though F-r-i-e-n-d would not fit in their real or mental form under the "relationship" section. I am, though, slightly irritated that I must answer these questions in the first place, fully content and satisfied with my response, feeling no need to explain myself further. (*CW*, August–September 1997)

ON A SWELTERING DAY in July 1997, I read the above, part of my attempt at a Maryhouse column, to Sister Jeanette. She, perched on her bed atop six, seven, or more blankets, clad in wool cap and sweater, and I, standing at the end of her bed, shaking at the possibility that she might reject me and my whole line about her. (Was I blowing her tough-as-nails, on top of barbed wire, on top of concrete, cover? Was this hokey? embarrassing? fair? honest?) She did not reject me. Maybe she should have corrected me on some things, but it is clear to me now that Sister, in our relationship, had great mercy on me. A mercy I surely did not deserve but am forever grateful for.

The bulk of Sister's life is a mystery to most of us who knew her. As told to us by Sylvia, Jeanette's sister, she came to New York City when she was sixteen years old. What hardships or blessings shaped her young life and built upon her impenetrable spirit, we do not know. She lived in an apartment on Ludlow Street for a good, long while. A poor person herself, this busy storm of a woman scavenged the streets and all over for clothing to bring to St. Joseph House. Whether the items found were even wanted or needed, it didn't matter. Sister Jeanette (as she introduced herself) began a relationship with the people in our houses, and it was her desire to salvage the bounty among us and distribute it to those she thought might be able to use it.

When her poor health made it impossible for her to maintain her own apartment, she moved into Maryhouse. We remember Sister Jeanette with her heaps of fan mail about her as she did her work. Her work was to filter through all of the causes she had supported and decide which of these would get a dollar or two. So generous was she that, despite a considerable cut in her monthly funds once she moved into the nursing home, Sister continued to offer small gifts to a few people every so often. We were decidedly humbled by her offer to provide the weekly money to buy bacon for everyone at Maryhouse—a treat she would have gladly partaken in but, sadly, could not. Throughout her life, Sister tended to the weakest among us in a way that was all her own. From the chunks of bread scattered behind and in front of Maryhouse as pigeon, squirrel, and definitely rat buffet, to her embrace and her mourning at the loss of her dear cat, Fluffy, Sister was generous with every bit of herself.

So many times, many of us at Maryhouse made endless efforts to persuade Sister to eat healthier, avoid the bacon fat and mounds of sugar that made up her breakfast, lunch, and dinner. In response, she would turn to me with a deep and threatening look, that look that made me want to shrink inside myself for fear of what might come. The chest of her sweater bedazzled with medals, miraculous and otherwise, gleamed at me—including a black and red button that read, "Not a Single Inch to Fascism!" Indeed, I had one foot in, and quickly, I wanted to retract it.

Sister Jeanette Chin died at Cabrini Hospital, in the early morning hours, on June 29, 2001. For the last four years, Sister Jeanette had been living at the Cabrini Center for Nursing and Rehabilitation, where she was cared for by the nursing staff with tenderness and compassion. On many occasions, I would come into her room and Sister, walker in hand, would rise and leave the room. She would walk into the dining room where I would hand her some deli cheese or liverwurst, her favorite contraband. If we were ever put off by Sister's apparent disregard for our visits or her silence, especially if we hadn't been there in awhile, we were usually consoled by the speed at which she devoured our treats. Sometimes, even an "I love ya!" passed her lips and brushed past my ears as I walked out the door.

O dear one, I have got to say it now. Sister had a (sometimes hidden) affection for just about everyone. For instance, there was her boy John, her boy Kerry, and her father Frank. I was Young Girl, and there was Momma Kassie and Janey Waney. Sister tugged on our Catholic Worker heartstrings with one line that rang true for her, and when we are trying our very best, hopefully, for us: "I vote for Jesus, because Jesus votes for everybody." She belonged to the (dis)order of the Catholic Worker, sometimes ministering to the holy chaos around the house and, a lot of times, stirring it up. She was our Sister, who in all of her days celebrated the delicate and knotty kinship among us.

At Sister's burial, the raw and wild earth opened up to welcome her at Silver Mount Cemetery on Staten Island. The gravediggers stood in the background, their figures making shadows with the trees. The sight was a compliment to Sister's full life, to the unequivocal strength of her will, to the enigmatic teacher she was to me, and to the eternal peace with which she now rests. "My soul is thirsting for the living God, when shall I see God face to face?" (Psalm 42:2), we responded at Sister's memorial. And oh, would I love to be a fly on the wall at that bound-to-be-raucous and joyous encounter.

Now, I read through that house column of my relationship with Sister Jeanette, as I described it, and I wonder how naive and presumptuous I was to call us friends after only two months of knowing each other. Certainly I wanted to be good to Sister, to support her and to care for her. I can only hope that sometime since then, if ever, I lived up to the weight of those words. To our Sister, we miss you and we long to see you again face to face.

St. Joseph House, 36 East 1st Street (1968–present)

Artist: Gary Donatelli

Mr. Wong (1921–2002)

BY MATT VOGEL

The Catholic Worker January–February 2003

IN AUGUST, MR. WONG celebrated his eighty-first birthday. As small and thin as he was, it was amazing that he was in such good shape for eighty-one. No health problems or complaints, nothing. When he did go to the doctor in September because he was having serious problems with his sight, Mr. Wong said that visit was his first—ever. As he kept telling the doctors, "I'm eighty-one years old! First time to the doctor. Not bad!" But, though still quite strong, it was clear that Mr. Wong was getting more and more frail and had lost a good deal of weight over the past couple of years. During the next few months, Mr. Wong had many, many appointments with quite a few doctors, and it appeared to them that he was indeed fairly healthy for somebody his age. But, on December 9, about a week after having cataract surgery to improve his sight in one eye, Mr. Wong died here at First Street—from heart disease, the doctors tell us.

To many of us—all of us, really—here at St. Joseph House, Mr. Wong was a complete enigma. Questions abound about him: Where did he come from? Did he work? What did he do? What about his family? What does he do, where does he go, when he goes out? People would even joke about how long it might take somebody new to figure out that, yes, in fact, Mr. Wong does live here. We know very little about his life outside the Worker for the past almost thirty-five years and even less about his life before he came to the Catholic Worker. What little we do know, we've gleaned from his time here inside the house and from those short conversations had here and there— short, mostly because nobody could really decipher his speech.

Mr. Wong was able to find—even create—privacy in a house known for its lack thereof. He was able to live his own life, share those parts of it he wanted known, and keep the rest. It is quite amazing actually, both in a world today where it can all too easily seem that even the most remote parts of our lives are open for public scrutiny, and in a community where everyone seems to know everybody's story and is not afraid to ask. Nobody can say the reason for such secrecy, but the fact that he managed it for nearly thirty-five years is pretty impressive.

What do we know? Well, according to Mr. Wong, he was born Wong Wah in China on August 30, 1921. In 1925, he and his family—he only mentioned his parents, Wong Sun, his father, and Wong Lee, his mother—came to the United States. They arrived from China in Vancouver, British Columbia, then took a train across Canada to Montreal, then another from Montreal to New York City. Mr. Wong—who took the name Tommy once in the United States—had lived in New York since then, in Chinatown and on the Lower East Side. He claimed to have worked in grocery stores, restaurants, and other small businesses, and hinted that he just may have owned a few himself.

He did live on Chrystie Street, right next door to the Worker, it seems, before the Worker (and him with it) moved to First Street. Since 1968, Mr. Wong had lived at 36 East First Street. House columns from the late sixties speak of Mr. Wong (along with Whiskers, among others), calling him a "steady waiter" on the soup line (*CW*, November 1968), and hint at his mystery: "Wong (called 'One Lung' by Italian Mike) silently watching his table as he presses (instead of rolling) a cigarette before waiting on another man." (*CW*, September 1968) It is not at all hard to imagine him standing there, watching the table closely out of the corner of his eye as he ever-so-carefully puts together one of his legendary spindly little cigarettes! In June of 1969, his prowess as a "waiter" and this same mystery are rolled into one in a fantastic description: "Wong serves his table with imperturbable aloofness and finesse that the volunteers have yet to equal."

At some point, however, it seems that Mr. Wong was ready for a new challenge, and was "promoted" to working on the paper. The first mention of him working on the paper is in the house column of February 1971. It seems that Mr. Wong, like many in the house at that time, worked on the paper steadily for several hours every day until the entire operation was moved to Maryhouse in the late eighties. Always a worker, that Mr. Wong, always a hard worker.

In his "retirement," Mr. Wong may not have even been retired! Some speculate that he may still have had jobs in Chinatown, but who knows? After he stopped working on the paper, Mr. Wong would go on walks, sometimes bringing back a duck or two (plucked, of course), tinker with his radios, often while listening to the Chinese-language station (Mr. Wong spoke a dialect of Cantonese); and, of course, he was always feeding the pigeons, and often the cats, too.

Despite the fact that he and his life were pretty much unknown, his absence is certainly noticed at St. Joseph House. Mr. Wong had a wonderful (and often crotchety) sense of humor. Whenever he came down from his room, he would crack jokes and make faces at nearly everybody else around him, teasing them about putting them in the soup, or dumping them in the East River. He'd stand there, usually near the front of the house, often facing the kitchen, with one hand on his hip, and smoke and watch, and watch, and watch. For being as private as he was, he knew what was going on. "You think I don't know?" he'd say, "I know," nodding his head.

But now he's just not there. He died on the third floor here at St. Joseph House and he is missed. Though he could be quite acerbic, often saying that both St. Joseph House and Maryhouse are "nuthouses" and calling us all "bums," Mr. Wong could be very sweet and tender in ways that didn't require words. A hug after a particularly difficult time, a smile in thanks for a small favor, watching out for somebody's bag, signing a birthday card, even speaking in perfectly clear, intelligible English to one's family—all showed a different Mr. Wong. Mr. Wong's entrance into the medical system must have been fraught with uncertainty for him, and he handled it as he handled the soup line, with "imperturbable aloofness." But, every now and then, with a questioning sideways glance, Mr. Wong would show his doubt, his fear, his vulnerability. These occasional forays into kindheartedness and weakness complicated and deepened that mystery that was Mr. Wong so much more.

So, we never knew Mr. Wong, really, and yet we did, and he is and will always be our brother. We laid this brother to rest yesterday, a clear, but quite cold day, underneath the bare trees on Staten Island, amidst the leaves covering the ground. It was quiet, so quiet, as we prayed from the Office for the Dead. Take it easy, Mr. Wong, take it easy.

Mattie Robinson

BY TANYA THERIAULT

The Catholic Worker August–September 2004

WE KNEW MATTIE BECAUSE he was our neighbor, since 1972, across the street at 31 East First Street. His parents, Annie and Joseph, lived on Sixth Street and were parishioners at Most Holy Redeemer, the church on Third Street, "Most Holy Madeema" in Mattie's parlance. It seems that, after their deaths, Mattie moved to our block and rarely left it, with one regular exception, to go to his job. We remember Mattie steadily weaving between the north and south sides of First Street with a childlike, toothless grin, many of the hairs on his head standing at attention, determinedly hauling trash, furniture and art on and off sidewalks, in and out of buildings. Mattie was not tall, nor hulking, but strong and lean. Led by a heavy and wide brow, he walked with a stomp. He had dentures but rarely wore them, and when he did that awkward fact was apparent. His hands wore rough calluses on the palms, evidence of his readiness for hard manual labor.

Mattie worked a union job as a janitor in an office building in Midtown. He wore a uniform and often worked the night shift. Who knows how it happened, but the union kept that job for Mattie for a good part of his life. He was a loyal worker, hardly ever called in sick, that is, when he was actually feeling ill. Only when his vision became impaired and he began getting sick on the job did he have to stop working.

With this job Mattie could maintain his apartment, his only possession. He came close to losing it several times for not paying the rent. To save it, Mattie alternately made trips to "The Money Store" for high-interest loans, entered a bare-knuckled sparring match (he won), or convinced the local loan shark to lend him money. Only after he had gotten the money, or was in a pickle to return the borrowed money, did we hear about it—the full story was never revealed.

Mattie was generous with his money and with his time and space, generous even to his detriment. On several occasions, Mattie would surprise "the girls" or "the ladies" of our house with expensive gifts. "For Mother's Day," he'd say, and hand over a tray of dried fruits and candied nuts from Russ & Daughters or a tin of Perugina chocolates, usually at some time approximately near the holiday itself. Many a stray pet found food and shelter with Mattie, including a boa constrictor (this one was not exactly a stray) which did not eat cheaply. He promised never to bring it inside the house (and didn't!), but a few from our crowd freaked out and screamed when Mattie paraded the snake, looped around his arms and torso, up and down the block.

Over the course of our knowing him, Mattie invited many people, some though not all with drug addictions, to live with him. All were in need of a place to stay and Mattie had them in. "Mattie Robinson, Friend of the Drug Addict!" a person from our house used to bellow. True, and it should be true of us all. Some took advantage of Mattie and many times he knew it. It was a mystery how these relationships worked out, as Mattie, to our knowledge, didn't use drugs. Some didn't work out, as manifested by shouting matches on the sidewalk or in the street between Mattie and whomever.

Mattie obsessed over his apartment during all of his lengthy hospital stays. It was where he wanted to be, to stay and, at times he'd say, to die. So strong was his desire to be in that apartment that it led to the Great Easter Escape. We asked Mattie if he wanted to come to the house for dinner on Easter Sunday. He was at Rivington House, a nursing/rehab facility for people with AIDS, just a few blocks away from the house. We picked him up in a wheelchair. Mattie ate a lot that night and was grateful for the getaway. But the getaway got farther away than some of us would have liked. Sometime between dinner and dessert, Mattie disappeared. With some help, Mattie made his way across the street and up to his third-floor apartment. In Mattie's mind, all that separated him from his apartment was not his need for medical care, and not the fact that he couldn't walk, but only First Street, a patch of tar that he knew with every step.

For many years, Mattie was the super for up to three buildings on the block. Whiskers recalls, "He was one of the captains of the block, which means that he helped clean up the block. He watched out for his neighbors." Without hesitation, Mattie helped us to haul tables and chairs, clearing out our kitchen for May Day or the Easter Vigil. In our kitchen, there hangs sheet metal behind the stove and a hood over the top. One evening, I had begun the task of trying to clean it, bit by bit. Mattie saw me at work and joined in. Soon, it was late and I went to bed. Mattie stayed and stayed through the night scrubbing and scrubbing. By morning, it shone anew. When someone graffitied the brick front of our house, Mattie went at it with nothing but soapy water and steel wool until it was gone. He watched out for us.

As Tiny, a longtime neighbor and friend from across the street, said, "If Mattie liked you he would do anything for you." One of the ways Mattie showed his affection for people on the block was by letting them use the abandoned lot next to his building, "Mattie's yard." Mattie would clean out the yard, making way for birthday parties, holidays, Whiskers' art shows, baptisms, and Rose's annual all-day buffet, open to the neighborhood, in honor of her saints. Tony Gawron painted a beautiful mural of St. Joseph the Worker on the eastern wall of the yard. Mattie's yard was a place for the neighborhood to gather and celebrate.

At other times, Mattie's yard was a spot where Mattie transformed other people's trash into art. There, a haphazard, multilevel structure displayed stuffed animals, potted plants, street signs, plastic flowers, mirrors, whatever. Two seven-foot-tall wood pillars stood prominently in most of his exhibits. One had a bust atop that resembled Malcolm X—Mattie swore that it was "dropped off by Malcolm's people." It was not unusual for passersby to ask, "Who is the artist?" Mattie didn't think of himself as an artist. He built it until it was done, until it was within his bounds of the beautiful.

Mattie was animated, a wild ride of a storyteller with a bent towards the fantastical. He would walk into the kitchen, pour himself a cup of coffee and, like one who tends a fire, Mattie would poke and prod, stoking the conversation to chaotic levels. In top volume, Mattie might begin the day by telling of his last night's dream. Undoubtedly it included a battle between Satan and any powers of good, God, Jesus, and the angels, involved in a tug of war for Mattie's soul. Regularly, Mattie popped by our house offering tidbits of unreliable gossip about folks on the block or those sitting across the table from him at dinner. The scene of fuel and fodder rolling through the rumor mill of First Street tickled him. If is was beef stew night, a meal he particularly detested, he might scream out, "Eww, this tastes like it's rotten!" "Mattie! It does not!!" a few might let out, principally the cook.

During one hospital stay, Mattie recounted the visions he had during the night. Arthur J. Lacey, Preston Lewis, and Tommy Masciotta, all now blessed memories of the Catholic Worker family, gathered around him. He was not frightened by their presence, but instead inspired to tell stories about Arthur, the "Bishop," calling folks to evening prayer, inviting Mattie to a quiet, holy time, as he described it. Mattie chuckled at the memory of Arthur's frustration with the slow pace and syncopation of fellow prayers around the table. Without his own family contacts, past generations of neighborhood friends filled Mattie's memories.

On February 6, a drizzling Friday afternoon, Matthais Robinson died in the hospice of Beth Israel Hospital. His hands rested upon his chest, his breathing was loud and labored, his skin was tight, grown thin and grey, and still Mattie hardly seemed his age of sixty years. Mattie had AIDS, a disease that within the last few years eroded his body down to its frame and finally took away his ability to work and walk. So disinterested in entering into the medical fray was Mattie that, when sick, he often reported treating himself to a raw egg and antibiotics shake; the antibiotics were surely a black market purchase.

In truth, Mattie can hardly be described without sounding like a mythical figure. Anyone who knew Mattie has a grab bag chock full of funny (only in the past tense and only if you're into dark humor), frightening, endearing, and mostly unbelievable stories with Mattie as protagonist, as instigator. Mattie, God Blessed, who will believe us when we tell them of the time you lined up fireworks along our sidewalk, only to spit sparks onto the brick face and windows of the house? When you built an altar in memory of Tommy that stood in the street for three days? Or the time your boa constrictor ate Adele's rooster on the eve of its journey to Peter Maurin Farm? Or when you, on Whiskers' order, you alleged, with hacksaw clumsily in hand, shortened Whiskers' sandals (they were on his feet) to fit him, and swiftly proceeded to cut scrap wood for a bench you built around our front tree? But what is a myth for, really, if not to serve as a way of unfolding a view of this world, its cruelty, its insanity, and its beauty, half rumor, some truth? Mattie had a hold on this world by all of its sharp points. Mattie, you are missed here on First Street.

Jane Kesel

by Geoffrey Gneuhs

The Catholic Worker October–November 2004

*Deciding today whether I will go on vacation until July 10 circa. If I
don't return late June 30, or the following day, then I won't be back
until circa July 10. Have to be very cautious, because I can't take the
chance that my life will be ruined by well-intentioned Workers, who
in fact have only a superficial knowledge of my problems.*

    *If I am not back earlier maybe you can persuade Thelma to care
for the library. She has been doing this superbly for months.*

So wrote Jane Kesel in one of her innumerable—and inimitable—
memos written to me (and other Catholic Workers) in the late 1970s to the
mid-1990s. These memos, letters, notes were typed single-spaced and often
several pages long and give a bird's eye view of life at Maryhouse—untypical, and unique, as they depict life from the point of view of a resident, a
guest, one who did not volunteer to come.

The vacuities and vagaries of life brought Jane Kesel to Maryhouse on
May 19, 1976, shortly after the house had opened. Unlike the proverbial
guest who came to dinner, she never intended to stay as she was "planning
to relocate." But, as the excerpt above indicates, indecision and procrastina-
tion shadowed her.

Jane was born in 1921 in New York City, into an upper-class Jewish
family who lived in a townhouse on East Seventy-third Street. Her father
taught at Columbia and later at the New School for Social Research. She
attended the Dalton School and completed her studies at Vassar College.
As a teenager, she spent summers in Villeneuve-sur-Lot, a small village in
the Dordogne in southwest of France. She recalled taking the train from

Paris to Holland in September 1939 for her return voyage to America before the border was closed.

She married and had two children. For a while the family lived outside of Seattle on what had been a chicken farm. At night, the now free-range chickens would roost in the trees peering at you "with their green eyes glowing in the dark."

The marriage failed. With sardonic humor about a painful time (never one to feel sorry for herself, only once, with tears, did she speak in any detail of that "grim period"), she said of her husband and parents, "We didn't see eye to eye." She spent some time, involuntarily, in a hospital, and then supported herself doing secretarial work and living in a rooming house. Mugged in Central Park in 1975, she found her way eventually to Maryhouse.

A resourceful person, intelligent, cultured, and mercurial—Jane was fiercely independent and spoke her mind, to the annoyance of certain Workers. She was an adult and expected to be treated as such. She cared about her appearance, preferring autumn colors. She was an accomplished cook of the Julia Child school—"the more butter the better!"—and wouldn't hesitate giving culinary advice which some would resent. She was a great help to me, along with Margaret Murphy, at the big holiday meals (I kept hidden in the pantry a bottle of sherry for us)—although Jane in a pre-holiday memo would invariably beg off from coming down to help due to a "crisis" with a "certain Worker," she would show up anyway. She always cautioned against my desire to cook goose—"they're way too fatty."

Early on she assumed the role of "librarian," which she finally resigned long ago (one of many resignations over the years); it gave her a sense of participation with proprietary rights. In one extensive and detailed memo about the decrepit condition of the library, echoing Myrna Loy in the 1940s movie *Mr. Blanding Builds His Dream House*, she wrote: "The Workers might want to consider painting one wall a color slightly darker than the others . . . It would be a real extravagance to paint the whole room at this time." She expressed concern about fabric for the broken settee: "Fabric samples from a place in the Village that specializes in burlap. But there is no point deciding on color scheme, quite impossible, until a decision is made regarding which parts of the room are to be painted and what color . . . My opinion is not to spend money in recovering until it is decided what is to replace the settee . . . I think there is a certain graciousness to a settee (in front of the fireplace also) and an aura of relaxing that a settee suggests." Getting a memo like that always charmed me and made me smile.

On more serious concerns Jane could be a defender of others; she was particularly—and rightly so—concerned about Lena when she was prescribed the drug Prolixin. Jane railed that it would make her "supine"—it did—and that her "civil rights" were being violated. Another time, referring to Maryhouse as "the Institute," she voiced concern that Catholic Worker philosophy needed reform: "Some changes in Catholic Worker theory . . . is not getting the scrutiny it deserves."

Words like "crisis," "controversial," or "crisis pitch" were often in the introduction to her memos that dealt with her relations with people at Maryhouse. Of one worker she wrote: "I am using the passive resistance ploy of totally ignoring her!" Of others she commented that they were "psychiatric neophytes," accusing them of "intense psychiatric pressure to make a decision regarding my religious affiliation. I am personally not so hot about all these Machiavellian convolutions." Jane was not one to suffer fools lightly. "I am again reminded how seldom things here are what they appear to be on the surface." She composed a fifty-page memo on "housekeeping at Maryhouse," which she declared was "so controversial" and "devastating" that it would probably land her out on the front steps of Maryhouse—it didn't!

She wasn't impressed with a Halloween party where Workers were "gyrating in that autistic manner that presently goes by the way of dance."

Jane was a kind woman. She once went with me and Jeannette Noel on a hot, humid August day to Jacques Travers' house of hospitality in Brooklyn. Jacques was away in France and had asked me to cook one of the meals for his community of twelve. Before we could cook, we had to spend about five hours cleaning the kitchen and defrosting the refrigerator, which wouldn't close for the bulging ice. After seeing that kitchen and house, Maryhouse looked like the Plaza Hotel. Another time she submitted a very fine list of speakers and topics for the Friday Night Meetings.

Her proverbially troubled "relations (non-relations would be more accurate)" with people at Maryhouse extended to the neighboring police precinct: "that Ninth Precinct, whose relations with me I have had rather serious cause to criticize"—though she gave no details.

Indeed, one of her great crises—as it was for any of us who were so attacked—came from scabies and lice. This ongoing crisis was the topic of several memos. She noted that she "came from a fashion-conscious background" and had never had such a problem before in her life. She complained that Helgi and "Scratchy" Annie received better head examination from certain Workers than she had. "I mean a louse is a louse and is no respecter of victim."

Her memos detailed squabbles with, among others, Juliana, Paulette, Katie, Dorothy Brewer, Hungarian Anna, and Elinore. Of the latter: "Outsiders also would find it difficult to imagine Elinore's carrying on, in which she yells at half a dozen persons in the course of a typical day here, and so would have difficulty getting the situation in perspective." Indeed, they would! She observed that "Katie Campbell sits in front of Maryhouse stretching out her hand at intervals to every passerby, and while not cursing the men donors, nevertheless making remarks that indicate their lack of generosity." She then opined, "I am inclined to believe the police will raid Maryhouse one of these days re: such matters as the above and the Workers will attain their wish that all the guests here or most of them will be carted off to Bellevue for involuntary examinations," concluding, "I wish to take every means to disassociate myself with these matters that seem to be disgraceful, and with the Worker movement, NYC."

Jane believed in the American sport of litigation, of suing, although her efforts never went much further than her typing. She would compose affidavits and prepare to file certain papers and documents. At some point in her life, she had refused a remittance from her family—it had "become increasingly inadequate"—in order to receive what she considered her share of her parents' estate. Like the case of *Jarndyce v. Jarndyce* in Dickens's novel *Bleak House*, the years went by and nothing came of it.

At one period, she asked if she could use my address for mail and would also come over to use my phone, "calls to the Israeli consulate (no, I have no plans to emigrate)," among others; other times we would have "high tea." Once we lunched at McSorley's Ale House, the oldest pub in New York. She was always going to take us to City Island to one of its fish restaurants for our August birthdays, but there was always a last minute excuse not to go.

Throughout the years, however, Jane suddenly would break off contact, and even wear a note pinned to her blouse, stating with her directness: "No contact!" One memo she signed, "Amicably (at least temporarily), J.K." One time she wrote, "I need a good dose of aloneness."

The June morning she went to the hospital for the last time (she stormed out of several hospitals when she felt she was not getting the right food and care she wanted), besides mentioning a few Workers she liked and approved of, she quoted a few lines from Shakespeare's *Julius Caesar*, a speech, she said, her father knew by heart. To the end, Jane retained a certain sophisticated, old-world class. Sociable but contrary, she remained a very private person. She was never dull, was always a good conversationalist, and, as has been said, had spunk.

Jane came to Maryhouse but was never going to stay, even after twenty-eight years; she was always planning to move, to relocate, to Venice, or maybe Paris, or maybe a "small town in New England," or maybe Florida. Maybe.

Clarice Adams

Artist: Sarah Brook

Clarice Adams (1925–2004)

BY JOANNE KENNEDY

The Catholic Worker December 2004

CLARICE CORNELL ADAMS DIED on Friday, June 13, 2004, at the age of seventy-nine. Claire, as she was known to us, was a woman of few words. When we told friends in the neighborhood that she had died, it was perhaps hard for them to recall her, as she spent the last six years of her life on the second floor of Maryhouse, her eyes, lungs, and legs no longer able to sustain her well going up and down the stairs. But it took only one phrase to jog their memories. She used to sit on the stoop next door and in her distinctive voice inquire, "Gotta cigarette?" Any denizen of Third Street could immediately conjure the image of Claire on that stoop. Many different people imitate her voice. It was gravelly, indeed it had a pebbly texture, but Claire also had a profound hearing impairment brought on by an inner ear infection in her childhood, and so, understandably, spoke in a very loud voice. In order to be heard by her, you had to speak loudly, very close to her ear, especially if you were trying to tell her something she didn't particularly want to hear.

She was a great devotee of coffee. "I want a cuppa coffee," would certainly be the second most common phrase on her lips. Margaret told a great story of a brutally hot summer day with Claire seated at her regular post in the dining room (first table on the right just inside the double doors), head down on her hands on the table. Margaret was worried for her in the stifling heat and asked if she'd like a drink. Claire answered in the affirmative, so Margaret presented a refreshingly cool glass of water. Claire took one small sip and said, rather indignantly, "That's water!" It was always hot coffee, no matter the weather. Hot tea would sometimes suffice. In later years, she was sustained primarily on Ensure, which she always called "Le'sure." And there were donuts and the occasional salami when she requested it.

The details of Claire's life were never terribly clear to most of us. She wasn't one to dwell on the past or even reminisce. Perhaps we didn't ask often enough. We know that she had been a child actor on Broadway. Felton managed to round up a couple of cast lists from two shows in the late 1930s that she had been in. He even found a musical number from the "The Angel Band," and we sang it around the Vespers table one night shortly after she died. Both shows seemed to have short runs, but that didn't diminish her star quality in our house. Claire maintained a devotion to the great movie stars of her day, commenting on their glamorous style. Who was her favorite? Was it Greta Garbo or Bette Davis? They did somehow seem like old friends or colleagues in her memory.

We know she married James Sherwood Adams, but that he died less than a year after their wedding. She always said, "He was a good man." She went to live with her sister, Dolores, at some point, here in the neighborhood. That relationship was difficult, fraught with the agonies of alcohol abuse, the anguish of so many families. Claire did seem to be haunted by memories of her sister. When Dolores died, Claire joined our family at Maryhouse.

While her eyesight allowed, she was a voracious reader; mysteries were her favorite. And she made short work of them. Those who have been around longer than others remember Claire as the so-called "runner." That is to say, she used to go to the corner deli for other women less able-bodied than she, no doubt procuring cigarettes along the way.

It seems trite to say it, but Claire was cute. She was short-statured and somewhat diminutive, but it wasn't that. She wasn't effusive or bubbly. A terse but heartfelt "thank you" was usually all you got. But she would occasionally have these sparkling moments of revelation that made your heart soar—glimpses of some part of her life as it had been (a few lines from a favorite song), or as it was ("Sometimes I get lonely"). Even the visiting doctors and nurses and physical therapists could not keep from commenting how delightful she was while she was trying not to cooperate with them. Perhaps they appreciated her lack of interest in their interesting questions and pesky procedures and her brilliantly frank discourse: "No, I don't wanna."

Others in Claire's situation might have found it humiliating. But she was never weighed down by that sort of pride which keeps us from accepting help. She endured each new person that came along, learning to provide her with the most intimate of care, with an albeit somewhat unconcerned patience. She rarely complained. One night when she had fallen getting back into bed and had broken her arm at the shoulder, all she said was, "My arm hurts."

Though her vision and hearing and memory so failed her that you might think she couldn't tell the difference between people, it was not true. She never got the names quite right, she probably never heard them correctly in the first place, but she could usually tell people apart. She never mistook Dee for Mary Griffin, who were both great friends to her for so many years. She knew we had different styles and mannerisms. She knew she could cheat on the nebulizer, which was easier with Roger than with others. She called Jonah "Jack," but she was consistent. Three days before her death, she asked about Jane's family while they were together.

In the last years, when she was feeling energetic and needed something, a cup of coffee usually, she would totter to her doorway and yell, "Cathy, Cathy, Cathy, Claire, Claire, Claire!" And we were all Cathy. At other times, she would exclaim, "I've been waiting for you," and she meant you. She would periodically ask to be awakened at eleven a.m. so she could get to "an important appointment" only to forget about it the next day. She would never say what the appointment was about—she played some cards close to her chest.

Claire taught us a lot about living our lives. Was she passive, or had she accepted her life in a way that few of us can? She allowed us to gently care for her, and by doing so, she cared for us, and perhaps we all cared for each other a little better. While we remember and wonder at her life, she is at the heavenly banquet, drinking coffee, smoking cigarettes, and finally taking care of that appointment.

Erich Probst (1933–2005)

BY JOE AND SABRA MCKENZIE-HAMILTON

The Catholic Worker March–April 2006

WE CAME TO KNOW Erich Probst shortly after we were married at St. Joe's in the spring of 1993. Roger knew him for some time before that, as part of a crew of physically huge, old-time Bowery Boys who were stumbling into sobriety. When we returned from our honeymoon, Erich was living at St. Joe's.

In a short time, he evolved into a father figure for many in the house, a patriarch in the best sense of the word. This began with a regular presence in the kitchen. A tall, broad-shouldered man with dark glasses, he would observe with his one, keen eye how the evening meal was prepared. It was clear that he had extensive experience as a cook in a previous life and had no reservations about sharing his knowledge. He was at once a demanding and an encouraging teacher, who was honest and didn't sugarcoat his opinions. He wasn't cruel, but let you know when things did not quite work. For as long as his health permitted, Erich's comments, techniques, and critiques came to be a common ingredient in most every meal prepared at the house. And he made them better.

Early on, he was also part of an ad hoc group that started a seemingly perpetual round of the card game spades in the kitchen. Recalling the many rotating members of this afternoon event brings to mind several dear friends who are now of blessed memory, including Mattie Robinson and Tony Gawron. Erich was a regular and dominant figure in the games, an exacting bidder who held his current partner, whoever that was, to very high standards. He enjoyed the joking and light talk that peppered the games, but wasn't above expressing his utter incredulity at a misplayed hand. Though his frustration was real, there was always a hint of a smile in his exasperation. He was happy to teach the game to anyone who was interested, and like his cooking advice, could be complimentary and encouraging to even the worst player. For all the mutual grief-giving, the games were fun and fast-moving, more full of wisecracks than complaints, which made the long, busy afternoons more enjoyable for everyone.

He also loved to share his opinions on a variety of topics—politics, books, movies, and Eugene. Saturday movie nights at St. Joe's were a mainstay for many years, and included heated debates about violence in film and whether or not it was appropriate for public viewing in a community committed to nonviolence. We understand he often tormented his roommate Jim with his choice of entertainment. At the same time, Erich would thoughtfully turn down the volume on his television so Jim could do his evening prayers. Jim spoke fondly about Erich at his memorial as a wonderful and thoughtful roommate, a pattern which began when he lived with his first roommate, Mr. Wong. Joanne recounted stories about how Erich would travel daily to the local bodega and purchase a small pie for Mr. Wong. It was never clear when Mr. Wong consumed this offering, but it became a silent ritual of mutual respect and gratitude.

Erich was also proud about his service in the Korean War as a paratrooper. There were no sacred cows for Erich, no settled answers. In our experience, he wrestled with the pacifism of the Catholic Worker and would often poke fun at the peace movement, even as he seemed to appreciate more and more the value of nonviolent personalism. He witnessed first hand how the nonviolence of the Catholic Worker was rooted in the commitment to the dignity and value of all people, that all are worthy and welcome. He found meaning in the connections formed between desperate people, even for himself, in this new family of which he was part. Through the ups and downs of his various illnesses he grew to accept and trust the care, concern, and love of this community. And the community was faithful to him.

He also developed an unusual and profound devotion to Dorothy Day, believing her intercession had helped heal him of the cancer that tormented him physically and psychologically for the last years of his life. During these years he lived with constant and considerable pain that he endured with quiet dignity, even as he never denied his suffering. This really touched on who Erich was as a person, both tough and tender.

One of his most endearing qualities was his genuine interest in how a person really was. He would ask direct questions, listen carefully, and offer advice. He wanted to share his wisdom with others, and would do so without hesitation. Quite a number of us have both resisted and rested in his words over the years, knowing that whatever he offered came out of a place within himself that was heartfelt and true.

When our first child, Adam, was born, he took upon himself a kind of surrogate grandfather role. While we took house shifts, worked on the paper, or taught Confirmation classes at Nativity Church around the corner, he acted as one of Adam's first babysitters. His paternal instincts were irrepressible and we felt supreme confidence that our baby would be safe and protected in the arms of this gentle giant. Erich prevented Mr. Wong from his oft-repeated, jocular threat to throw Adam in the soup and was one of the first to witness our son take his first steps at the local playground.

Erich at once advocated that we be stern and consistent parents, even as he attempted to spoil our children. He always admonished us to love our kids and care for them attentively and strictly, even as he relentlessly lavished them with elaborate and thoughtful holiday and birthday gifts. These gifts, of course, were not without their humorous pokes at us as parents. He made stage-whispered comments about his intention to buy war planes and elaborate Disney toys. He never did, though he was always slyly pleased to see our reaction when the kids opened their gifts that inevitably had the loudest possible bells and whistles. The kids always loved these presents and happily played along with Erich's delight at our bemused dismay. That was Erich, stressing to us the importance of being lovingly tough on the kids as he was spoiling the daylights out of them.

The reality was that he loved children, all children. He had a special love for Georgie and Serene, for Sophia and Jonah, for Nicole and Brendan. His nightstand had an array of these children's pictures, displayed with a grandfather's pride. He never failed to ask after them and was always pleased by a visit. We often wondered why he had severed connections with his own children and his family of origin. At the same time, we realized he was with his family, a new family that he had adopted and who had adopted him.

How can we sum up the life of someone who had such numerous, significant relationships with others, and at the same time placed a shroud of mystery over his own history? While we do not know exactly the journey that brought Erich to the community, it was clear that a new chapter began for him at the Catholic Worker. Whatever brokenness there might have been gave way to the building of a new life, a new family, a new home. He walked through the doors of St. Joe's into a community where he could build real relationships with others, at a time in his life when he could be depended on and could depend on others. A community where he lived a sober life as a committed father figure and friend. When his wise heart finally gave out, the overflowing waiting room on the Beth Israel cardiac care floor was testament to a life of fullness lived in deep and faithful connection with others.

Venante Martin (1925–2006)

by Tanya Theriault and Matt Vogel

The Catholic Worker October–November 2006

TWO YEARS AGO, ONE Tuesday night after Mass, Venante Martin arrived from JFK Airport at St. Joseph House. She had just come from Haiti, having tried unsuccessfully to return to her home. We had been acquainted with Venante prior to her arrival through her nephew Yvon, who was a mainstay at St. Joe's for several years. His *Tante* (Aunt) Venante nursed him in her Brooklyn apartment as he grew more and more ill. After his death, she grew tired of living alone, her rent had gone up, and she surrendered her apartment for an attempt to live again in Haiti. For whatever reason—she told us it was medical, but she always added that Haiti was bad now, not like before, when she was growing up—she returned to the U.S. Venante now had no place to go, but she knew Carmen and Roger, so she came to St. Joseph House.

Venante first came to the U.S. on July 4, 1968, one year after her brother—Yvon's father, who was also named Yvon—was beaten to death by the *Tonton Macoute*, François "Papa Doc" Duvalier's notoriously brutal private militia. Haiti was being driven deep into the nightmare that was life under the Duvaliers and when some friends who had already come to the U.S. suggested that she come as well, she did. She worked without papers, mainly office and secretarial jobs, though also for a time as a nurse's aide, and sent money back to Haiti for the support of her brother Yvon's two children, Yvon and his sister, Colette.

Venante never married and had no children of her own. She would tell us that she sometimes thought she should have been a nun, but that she needed to support her family, so she could not enter the convent. So, it was fitting that her own birthday fell on November 1, the Feast of All Saints, with her great devotion to St. Thérèse of Lisieux (she never failed to mention that she and the Little Flower shared the same last name) and to St. Anthony of Padua. She had great faith in the Church and its holiness, but always recognized its humanity (both positively and negatively)—one of her favorite pictures that she had on her dresser was of an infant John Paul II, "the baby pope," she called it. She was glued to the TV and radio when John Paul II died, eagerly anticipating the new pope, updating all who passed by her bedside on the process, and stayed up all night with Eugene to watch Midnight Mass at the Vatican at Christmas. She never had her Bible (in French, of course) far from her, and when she was better able to get around, she was a daily communicant. She loved the Mass—the Scripture readings, the songs, the music, the incense, the prayers, mouthing the words along with the priest. More than anything, though, she had a strong and unshakeable relationship with Him Whom she called "my man"—Jesus Christ. These words from the autobiography of St. Thérèse so resonated with those of us who knew Venante when we gathered for Vespers the evening after her death: "Jesus, my love! At last, I have found my vocation. My vocation is love! I have found my special place in the Church, and that place, you, my God, have given me."

Beyond all these pious practices, she prayed seriously and had a very real conviction that God was present to her and acting in her life. When in the nursing home, she loved to receive Amanda's invitation to the weekly Sant'Egidio prayer, making a line from their prayer something of a mantra, "Where there is love, God is there." Far from sanctimonious, her faith was really a quiet, impenetrable strength, palpable to anyone who knew her. It was this inner strength, we think, that made her as tough as she was. Venante was a worker in the best and truest sense of the word, a trait she shared with Yvon, determinedly doing a job because it needed to be done, and doing it well.

Before the stroke that would leave her confined to the fourth floor for most of the day, she would help do the dishes after dinner. At seventy-nine years old, she'd ask only that you tie the apron on over her simple but always clean and classy clothes. At the sink, washing the dishes, the pots, the pans, patiently scrubbing away, changing the water when necessary, Venante would finish as spotless and dry as when she started. It was a testament to that toughness that when asked about a later physical therapy session, she'd often respond, "Good. They worked me hard." Initially, the damage from her stroke led doctors to believe that she might never walk again. She got strong enough to first walk twenty or thirty feet, then stronger still to return to St. Joe's, making a daily trip down from the fourth floor for dinner, and for weekly Mass, then back up again.

From the very beginning, Venante seemed to "get it," to innately understand the Catholic Worker, our work and our life together. Most of all, she understood hospitality and excelled at filling in what others in the house left out. We can do the major stuff fairly well, putting food out on the table, getting beds ready, and the like. But Venante would do those little extra things that made folks feel welcome, appreciated, and at home. She'd make sure that everyone had a napkin at dinner. She'd wake up early and make morning tea for guests on the fourth floor, and she'd make conversation, genuinely interested in you, your life, and your family—even when she didn't speak your language.

Not too long ago, we had a woman staying with us who spoke only Spanish. Venante could speak French, Haitian Creole, and English, but no Spanish. But she made a point of befriending this woman who was very far from home, staying in a strange place, and in stressful circumstances. Venante would sit with her all day, every day, tuned her radio to the all-Spanish news station, somehow found out about her family, her kids, and relayed her own story, helping this scared guest to feel more comfortable and less alone.

Venante had her regular pals as well. She sat next to Whiskers at dinner, watched afternoon television with the Genius, and took Joanne M. on her walks when she was able. She had a particularly soft spot for children. She was always asking about Jonah, wanting a complete report of any time spent with him. She loved to see pictures of schoolchildren in *Catholic New York*, the archdiocesan newspaper, and to call your attention to children playing in the street or babies being pushed down the sidewalk, taking everything in with great joy.

Given enough time with Venante, though, her compassion and courteousness weren't all you saw. She had a wicked sense of humor. She would crack jokes with not a little sarcasm, gently poking fun and teasing. When she was in the nursing home, if you didn't come often enough for her liking, she might blurt out "Four Days!" when you walked in to visit; it had been four days since you last came. Or, she might immediately close her eyes and look away, as if she wanted you to leave. She would often hold her (pseudo) angry stare or stay with her eyes closed just long enough for you to think she was seriously angry or hurt, and then she'd let loose a big smile and a deep laugh. Cunning and, at times, flirtatiously, she got you.

Though she was never rude, that smile could instantly vanish should you bring up something or suggest something contrary to what she had decided. Venante was quite stubborn, and once she made up her mind the topic was closed. It took some convincing to get her to go to St. Vincent's so late on the Friday night of her stroke, but she went. One time, we were discussing the possibility of her staying in the nursing home longer, for more physical therapy. In no uncertain terms she told us that she was not going to stay there, "Peer-i-aud," slowly drawing out the word and folding her arms across her chest. Well, that was that, Venante-1, Tanya and Matt-o.

She put in hundreds of hours of work attempting to regain lifelong skills of which her stroke robbed her. Three times a day, twenty repetitions per exercise; she was, at times, exhausted and increasingly frustrated and disappointed with her body's failings. Venante had had beautiful penmanship and was a great card writer, attentive to every birthday, holiday, and occasion in the house. She was embarrassed to have lost the ability to write clearly and tried to get it back, copying pages from *Catholic New York* and *The Long Loneliness*. She never was able to sign her name quite to her satisfaction, though she did not stop trying.

Even during this time when she needed so much help to do the things we all take for granted—bathing, getting dressed, writing a card, walking downstairs—she maintained her gracious gracefulness. Venante was always a lady, as one of her longtime friends said at her funeral, and this was certainly true. A later fall sent Venante back into the hospital and nursing home with a serious back injury and a great deal of pain in its wake. But still, at every visit, she worked to make you feel at home, sitting up and arranging herself, finding a place for you to sit and chatting about the comings and goings and health of everybody in the house.

The truth is that we only knew Venante for about two years. We didn't know the Venante who found a place to bury her brother, or the Marie Venante Martin who was baptized in Petit-Goâve, Haiti, or the Venante who was kept on at the NYC Board of Education even after she was told people without papers couldn't work there, a piece of her work history of which she was quite proud. We didn't know Venante when she lost her mother at twenty-three, and was embraced in a vision by St. Thérèse, or the Venante who taught typing in Papa Doc's Haiti. But, in a sense, we did. We saw, quickly and clearly, her dedication to doing the right thing, regardless of an available, easier way; her strong work ethic; her compassion for anyone in need; her keen sense of her own dignity; her sense of humor and innocent teasing; her love of Haiti and the Church; and her deep and sincere desire to be with and follow Jesus. A friend told us at her funeral that she really was always like that—she had no wayward youth or anything of that sort—always, just like that.

Petit à petit, l'oiseau fait son nid—little by little, the bird makes her nest—she offered in an exchange about English- and French-language proverbs, and it describes her time with us well. Little by little, she built a life here, until it seemed as though she'd been with us for much longer than she had. Little by little she built a nest in our hearts—we are truly lacking without her. Dorothy Day used to quote Dostoevsky, saying that "beauty will save the world." If so, it is the beauty of those like Venante that will save us all. À *bientôt, Madame, à bientôt.*

Natale Pace (1935–2006)

BY SIOBHAN O'NEIL

The Catholic Worker January–February 2007

I DEFY ANYONE TO recall a time when Nat Pace was mean or belittling to any living thing. Was Nat peculiar? Eccentric? Superstitious and consumed with all practices magical? This goes without saying. Was he liable to be sneaking ice cream despite having diabetes; prone to annoy roommates with his incessant nocturnal pacing (during his first years at St. Joe's); capable of letting loose unworldly and seemingly uncontrollable guttural howls at any hour of the day or night? Was he puffing on three cigarettes simultaneously during his last days at St. Joe's? Yes—all these are true. But the more essential truth is that Nat Pace was a sweet, kind-hearted, generous, gentle, peaceful, serene, quizzical soul. Many believe that it was not an accident that he was born on Valentine's Day, and was given the name Natale Pace, which translates from the Italian as peaceful birth, peaceful Nativity.

Although much about Nat's life and early history with the Catholic Worker is a bit vague, to the best of the collective Catholic Worker memory, Nat first came to the Worker in the late 1980s. At the time, he was living in a hotel on the Bowery. Nat moved into the Worker in 1990 or 1991. Matt and Tanya recall hearing that, having been robbed of his disability check, Nat could not pay his rent and became homeless. He temporarily stayed at the men's shelter at the Holy Name Centre before moving onto the second floor of St. Joe's, where he lived for much of the rest of his life.

If Nat's history is a little hazy, his unique disposition—so generous and so peculiar—is the stuff of legend. Perhaps his absorption in all matters magical and his obsession with superstitious practices inspired Nat, from even his first day at St. Joe's, to quietly and with a conjurer's sleight of hand get ahold of more than a dozen paper cups, fill them with various but precise amounts of water and then place them around the kitchen, in what the yet-to-be-initiated saw only as a very consistent, asymmetrical pattern. At the time, paper cups were a guarded commodity. Yet, somehow, day after day, no matter how carefully we hid them and no matter how many time we tossed out the ones Nat placed around the room, the cups would eerily reappear on the kitchen tables in the same configuration.

A similar collection of cups appeared around his bed and personal space. Whether Nat was creating some kind of circle of protection, for himself or the house, or whether we were all unknowing participants in some elaborate ritual touching on the supernatural, or whether Nat's placement of cups actually helped to assure the proper order of house and universe—we were never certain. But we came to realize that since this distribution of cups throughout the house was necessary for Nat and all efforts to thwart his activity were doomed to failure, we might as well accept it as one accepts the cycle of the moon or the existence of wizards. Over time, the cups became a normal, predictable, and almost comforting part of our life at St. Joe's.

Nat had a number of odd, inscrutable, yet endearing habits. He tended to keep twenty or so pens and an assortment of rubber bands in the front pocket of his white buttoned-down dress shirts (the pens came in handy as there was never one to be found in the kitchen of St. Joe's) and a couple of hangers in the back of a coat draped over his shoulders. He was often loaded down with heavy plastic shopping bags, so much so that he used leather straps to support his wrists. However, there was something dashing about him in his formal dress shirts, with his full head of white and black hair, his whimsical smile and husky chuckle. Nat could not hide that he knew he was a good-looking guy and clearly he felt, or possibly even believed, that he was years younger than his actual age. On numerous occasions, when asked how old he was by a younger woman, Nat would without hesitation knock a few decades off his age.

Nat's debonair qualities were perhaps best displayed during Vespers at St. Joe's back in the years when Arthur Lacey, the Bishop of the Bowery, presided over the nightly holy recitations. Nat had, in general, a very sweet warm voice. Yet aside from the occasional howl or spasmodic grunt, he was often silent, lost in some mysterious reverie. But during evening prayers, Nat's gift for the dramatic was on full display. Although impossible to note on paper, at Nat's memorial Mass, Jane Sammon managed an uncannily accurate imitation of Nat's emphatic, yet melodic, voice from Olympus—his unintentional, sing-song parody of a poet's diction.

As many of us rushed and mumbled through Vespers, Nat would wring every nuance out of a word and bring to life every phrase in a pace set to some internal metronome. This talent of Nat's was mesmerizing to all with one glaring exception: It drove Arthur mad! Arthur would rap his colossal ring on the table, voice a string of corrections and reprimands, and attempt to restore a sense of decorum to the proceedings. His efforts were to no avail, for Nat never hurried or altered his signature phrasing. Nat didn't mind being scolded by Arthur for always being a line or two behind the rest of us in the recitation of the Our Father or the Magnificat. He was too absorbed in relishing every line and exploring each phrase to notice such worldly protests.

In general, Nat took life at a fairly leisurely pace. He regularly went to Maryhouse to help fold the paper, embarked on long, meandering walks, and enjoyed drawing intricate pictures that were inspired by his interest in wizardry, fantasy, and the supernatural. Although Nat's kind, generous nature and peaceful demeanor were a constant, his physical condition was permanently altered by a stroke in 1994. Up until that time, Nat had done his best to avoid medicine, doctors, and hospitals altogether. This inclination made it very difficult for us to convince him to seek medical care after his stroke and it was several days before we finally got him to the hospital. While at the hospital, he continued to be resistant to medication and treatment for what we came to learn was diabetes, which had led to a stroke. Yet, over the month or so that he spent there, Nat relented and began taking medicine and some notice of his physician's advice. When he returned to St. Joe's, Nat, with some not so subtle persuasion, continued to take his medicine and often willingly went to appointments with physical therapists, dietitians, and other medical specialists. Soon after his return home, Nat came under the care of a series of home health care attendants. Hector Perez and Julia Lewis stand out for their longevity, excellent care, and abundant acts of kindness to Nat.

The most dramatic change in Nat's life that resulted from his stroke was how immobile he became. No longer a pacer, he became reluctant to go downstairs, let alone go for a walk. Nat became confined to the second floor. Getting downstairs to the kitchen became such a major undertaking for Nat and such a rare event that inhabitants of the kitchen would break into spontaneous applause at the mere sight of him at the door. We encouraged such sightings as much as possible by attempting to ban everyone from bringing his dinner plate or other food up to him in bed. After I moved out of the house, the one, sole benefit of his immobility was the guarantee he would be on the second floor when I came to visit. As was surely the case with everyone, Nat never failed to grant me a warm greeting, a dazzling smile, an endearing laugh and then proceed to shower me, as well as everyone who had ever lived or still lived in the house, with compliments and gratitude for all the hard work and kind acts we had done on his behalf and on behalf of the Catholic Worker. Yes, Nat Pace was a charmer.

The other major challenge for Nat was to avoid eating anything with sugar, or rather, avoid being caught with sugar, depending on your perspective. Nat had always been a very generous soul and after moving into the house he regularly offered tips, paid for take-out meals, and provided compensation to anyone who ran him an errand, or did him a perceived favor, or provided some service. His tendency to share his money was especially evident on check day, when Nat was apt to offer a few dollars to just about anyone walking by his bed. As Nat became less mobile and less able to get his hands on sweet, delicious things in the house, his need became more and more acute to have a number of willing and available runners to go to Roger's Garden (a local deli) on his behalf and then sneak controlled substances—cake, cookies, soda, ice cream—into the house and up to the second floor. Over time, he offered more and more incentives to those that risked such treacherous forays.

Although Nat did not often get off the second floor, on a few special occasions he was inspired to take center stage in the kitchen of St. Joe's. These occasions, which became known as The Nat Pace Show, were recalled with much enthusiasm and fondness at the memorial by folks who had lived in the house during the second half of the nineties. Although I didn't witness these happenings, Tanya related that the events were hosted by Jeremy Scahill and began with songs about Nat and the household to the tune of the Brady Bunch theme song, and usually took place on holidays. Nat would sit up in front wearing a wizard's hat and proceed to interview household members and guests on various topics supernatural. One of the most memorable shows took place on a Halloween night when Joanne, Lucia, and Tanya came dressed as the Holy Trinity. Nat drilled them about the end of the world. The third part of their prophecy has yet to be unsealed.

In 2003, Nat's health took a turn for the worse. His diabetes became uncontrollable and he had another stroke. After a prolonged stay in the hospital, Nat moved to the Cabrini Center for Nursing and Rehabilitation, where he resided for the last few years of his life. Tanya, Matt, Eugene, Amanda, and Jane were his most regular visitors. As his room was on the first floor, he often sat in the lobby ready to greet anyone from the house and immediately try to persuade them, Eugene especially, to go to the store to get him something sweet or a cherished pack of cigarettes. Brother Vishwas, who regularly offers Mass at St. Joe's on Tuesday evenings and presided over Nat's memorial there, became the chaplain at the Cabrini Center two years ago and became very close to Nat, spending the final days with him. In August 2006, Nat underwent an operation to amputate his leg, the result of his diabetes. He never fully recovered and spent much of the last few months of his life in bed.

At the memorial, Brother Vishwas remarked on the kind care Nat received from the staff at Cabrini and about their pleasure at hearing Nat's warm, pleasant voice. "Let us hear your soft sweet voice," one of the staff was heard to say. During the last days, the voice grew weaker with frequent requests for water. Although what was happening deep in his spirit was mysterious, what struck Brother Vishwas most during those final days was Nat's "peaceful serenity, his sweet smile." Mary Lathrop remarked at Nat's memorial service that it was fitting that Nat's name means "Christmas Peace" and that Nat died just before the start of Advent and the coming of the Infant's birth.

Christmas has passed and the New Year has come. Nat, may you be reborn in the Spirit, and may your thirst be quenched by the love of God. Rest in peace, dear Natale Pace.

Theodore Roosevelt Ridlon

BY TOM CORNELL

The Catholic Worker March–April 2007

SLIM SLIPPED AWAY IN the early afternoon on Thursday, January 4, at Peter Maurin Farm in Marlboro, New York. Theodore Roosevelt Ridlon was also known as Frank Bourne, and received Christmas cards so addressed. But to the townspeople of Marlboro he was "The Man Who Walks." They could not fail to note the lonely silent figure who trod with a slow steady gait the streets of this small town where, until recently, everybody knew everybody else. Slim was a tall man, well built, but bent slowly with age. He cut his own hair and beard, lately thin and white. His fashion set trends. Long before adolescent male trousers drooped with crotch almost to the knee, Slim perfected the style. Tom Murray suggested we buy him overalls. That solved the exposure problem. Then Slim took to wearing only one strap over his shoulder, the other dangling insouciantly. That caught on, too! On walks into town, when he tired, Slim stretched out wherever he was, by the road, in a shopping mall parking lot, once in a supermarket. The local police would drive him home if they found him thus. Usually he made it on his own. It has been a few years since he was able to walk more than the fifty or so yards between the houses here.

Slim had been with us at the farm in Tivoli and came to Marlboro when we relocated in 1979. Before that he lived at the old Peter Maurin Farm on Staten Island, before that at Maryfarm in Newburgh, before that at the farm in Easton, Pennsylvania, all the farms, in fact. When he first came to the Worker, Slim lived at the Mott Street house, but the crowds rattled his nerves, so it was decided that he would be better off in the country. For a brief while in the early fifties, Slim came back to the city, but was on edge there. Even here in Marlboro, if there was a retreat or a student work group, Slim would retire to his room and stay there until the guests had gone. Then he would take his place before the TV monitor and ask for a movie. We have acquired VHS versions of almost the entire John Wayne corpus. I first saw Slim sitting at the dining room table at Peter Maurin Farm on Staten Island, in his mid-thirties then, looking strong. He sat at that same table up until two months ago, now eighty-seven and clearly failing. It was congestive heart failure.

Roger O'Neil could coax him into fragments of conversation about the old days, but for the most part Slim answered a question in few words if any, and spoke mostly to his invisible friend in mumbles and hand gestures. Ralph Dowdy once asked him if he remembered Peter Maurin. "What was he like?" "He was a gentleman," came the answer. When he lived at the Tivoli farm, Slim was so quiet that Eileen Egan called him "Silent Slim," thinking him mute. Sheila Dugan recalled, "I never heard one word out of him, although he smiled at me a lot. Keiran, ignoring the fact that he never got much of a reply, carried on conversations with Slim and Slim would laugh and laugh. Norma Melbourne swore he was the most intelligent person she ever met, just didn't have patience for small talk and it was all small talk."

Johannah Hughes Turner remembers that young Martin John Corbin, Rita and Marty's son, when he was a preschooler, stayed by Slim's side for walks, at meals, and whenever and wherever he could. There was a bond there, real and good. Slim was a good and gentle man. Johannah writes, "Slim used to talk with me and my brother Tom when we were teenagers living on the original Peter Maurin Farm on Staten Island. Mostly it would be brief commentary on baseball or items in the *Daily News*. He read newspapers all the time. He was known to talk only occasionally at Tivoli. He appeared to be listening, most of the time, and often laughed to himself, probably at the personal and communal craziness swirling around him. It always struck me that he lived an incredibly lonely life, without physical contact and without much verbal contact, even with those who lived in the same house with him. Thanks to the people at the Marlboro farm for taking such good care of Slim in his last years. That attention to his needs, his feelings, his presence, was probably the best he had ever known." The credit for that must go first to Else and Ralph Dowdy, then to Barbara Lapidus and Tom Cornell the Younger.

The story of Slim's arrival at the Catholic Worker has a few variations. What I received is that his mother brought him to the Catholic Worker at Mott Street, said he was a good boy but mentally challenged (or whatever the thirties' euphemism was), and that he wouldn't cause any trouble and that she'd be back to get him Monday. That was in 1937. She left no identification papers, no contact information.

Ed Turner recalls that, when Slim lived at the Chrystie Street house on the Bowery, "he mostly stood in the upper hallway saying nothing. When they got him to the farm (on Staten Island) he jumped out of the car and rolled around on the grass for some time, and then became more talkative. At Chrystie Street he seemed to be in a catatonic state although he always responded when someone said hello to him."

Here, Slim had children and dogs around him. He had jobs. In the spring and fall he raked leaves, he hauled water, he took out the garbage. In the winter he shoveled snow, cutting paths between houses and then as his imagination led, pathways to utopia, you might say.

When asked, Slim gave his birth date as November 21, 1919. After more than two years' search, I found that he indeed had been born on that date in Randolph, Massachusetts, so that we could establish a legal identity for him. At one point I asked Slim if he was baptized, or if he wanted to be baptized. He said, "That won't be necessary, Tom Sir," his customary response. "Do you want a doctor to look at your hernia?" "That won't be necessary, Tom Sir." "Shall I scramble your eggs?" "Not at the moment, Tom Sir." Monica was still "Miss" after more than forty years, I still "Sir" after more than fifty. But he did tell me that he was a Catholic Christian. His mother must have told him that, and that must have been the reason why, when she decided to dump Slim at the legal age of eighteen, she gave him to us.

Slim had the full rites of the church. The Office for the Dead was said for him. Our pastor Father Ed Bader presided at Mass attended by Rita Corbin, Bob Steed, Alan Cerchia, Carol Campaign, Rita Oliver, Mary Glacken, Bud Courtney, John and Serene Good, Clare Danielsson, Bob Moritz, a dozen other friends, and our farm community. Slim was buried in consecrated ground with George Collins, Alice Erwin, Alice Lawrence, John Filigar, Harvey Hoffman, Cleophas Ezekiel Shortt, Charles Deans, Arthur Sullivan, Michael Malinowski, and James Lewis. May he rest in peace and rise in glory.

BY RALPH DOWDY

SLIM'S LIFE COULD EASILY be turned into a parallel story of the Catholic Worker's creation. If the stories could be told of the times, relatively short, we have lived with Slim at Peter Maurin Farm, it would be a medley of how the Catholic Worker bumped into the world of conformity on a daily basis. Of the modern criminal bureaucracy by which we are all oppressed, Slim was liberatingly unaware.

One Slim story: Once on a regular weekly trip of the Peter Maurin Farm gang to the ShopRite supermarket in Newburgh, Slim, who never went, was for some unknown reason invited to come for the ride. "Who will be with him?" someone asked, concerned that he would walk off and get lost. Slim was a true blue walking man, not to be stopped! So one of the old-timers, George Collins, who was as true as clockwork to his word, said, "I'll be with him."

So off the gang goes for the ten-mile food trip. Else, the driver, and, as usual, the mainstay leader of the gang, once in the store, was going down one aisle after the other checking item after item off her list. Suddenly she heard a loud, sharp woman's voice demanding, "Sir, you can't lay down there, you have to get up! Sir, you have to get up!" "Oh shit," Else said to herself, "I know who that is," as she went trucking to the nearby aisle to see, and sure enough, Slim was stretched out in full resting form in the middle of the aisle.

True to himself and the family he was in, Slim was tired and rested on the spot. George Collins, who had spent three years in prison as a conscientious objector, was not fazed in the least by such trivial family happenings, and with a friendly suggestion from Else walked with Slim to the van.

So in life, so in death, Slim was always easygoing. And personally, there is nowhere on God's good earth that I know of where Slim could have had the love and care he received from Barbara and Else and the Peter Maurin Farm folks.

Slim also gave so much to us in his mostly active silent presence that words cannot express it fully. His bodily presence is missed, his story is the stuff of Worker life.

Evelyn Dudley (1938–2008)

BY JOANNE KENNEDY

The Catholic Worker March–April 2008

EVELYN DUDLEY LIVED AT Maryhouse for roughly the past twelve years. She came to love the house, and in particular her work with the women at lunchtime over the years. She credited Margaret Murphy with instilling in her an understanding of life at Maryhouse and teaching her all the proverbial tricks of the trade. When Margaret died, Evelyn naturally stepped into what was the void that Margaret left. She began helping out at lunchtime by getting whatever special things folks asked for—"Evelyn, I need socks!" or toothpaste or deodorant. She nearly always managed to produce something that satisfied, and if not, she had a genuine apology which was usually accepted. Her reputation for success was so great that when she wasn't working, there was a palpable sense of disappointment among the lunch crowd. Though others were asked, expectations were usually low.

She was also notorious for her training regimen. Hardly a new volunteer over the past few years did not run the gauntlet with Evelyn. She really enjoyed showing folks the ropes and took great pride in watching them grow in the job. You never saw a broader grin than when one of Evelyn's "students" survived their first clothing room day on their own or, even better, managed to quell a fight or take care of a particularly unhappy person. The new volunteer usually experienced a day or two of overwhelming confusion which inevitably blossomed into comprehension and satisfaction. Evelyn, born in South Carolina and raised in New York City, had a particular affinity for our German volunteers and they for her. When she became seriously ill, there were no fewer than three folks we knew we had to call in Germany and there are many more who will no doubt be saddened to hear of her death.

Evelyn was a woman of great energy and stamina. Only when her illness progressed did one ever see sign of her actually growing tired or weary. In truth, you mostly became aware of it because she complained about being frustrated with not feeling like she could do as much work as she normally did. And her normal load was sometimes amazingly heavy, especially for a woman of her age. Joanne King, just the other day, as she was holding Evelyn's Mass card, commented that she looked much younger than her actual age. And that is indeed true. The omnipresent bandana or headscarf did a great job of hiding what grey hair she had, and her strength did the rest. Plus, she overflowed with life.

She had a great enthusiasm for the things in life that she enjoyed. Eugene recalled that she would talk gently to the plants she so dutifully watered and nurtured in the front and back and roof yards of the house, even calling them her babies. She was a fine cook, and many folks remember her cooking and sharing pig's knuckles and greens, or frying fish with Joe Wells, or the truly ambitious undertaking of making salmon croquettes for the whole lunch crowd. She clearly enjoyed good soul food and thought it was the cure for many ills.

She also loved music. On Sundays, it was always gospel music, but for mopping the floor, Motown was preferable. When James Brown died, she felt his loss in a deep way and even got on the bus to go up to Harlem to farewell him. Tina Turner was another favorite, but all the standards from the early days of Motown were most enjoyable, and she liked her music loud, the louder the better, whenever possible. On Friday nights, though, she liked to watch wrestling on television.

She had a super soft spot for kids and no amount of pleading could convince her to stop spoiling Jonah. If a donation of toys came in, she always set them aside for him and as soon as he got home from school she would give him the whole bag, not just his pick of the best. When she was out on the street shaking her cup collecting the generosity of others, she would invariably reach in without hesitation and hand Jonah a dollar when he walked by, and I think he wasn't the only recipient of her generosity.

In Evelyn's death, we had a great privilege of getting to know her family in a way we had not before. Two brothers and a sister as well as her two daughters, eight grandchildren, and three great-grandchildren survive her. The funeral home was standing room only on the day of visitation.

There were also lots of cousins and nieces and nephews and in-laws and friends. People got up to share thoughts and prayers of thanksgiving for her life. Many described her as a woman who didn't mince words, who told you exactly what was on her mind, even though that was sometimes hard to hear, but that she also really enjoyed laughing. Her brother called her Mabel, her children called her Frances, and to us she was Evelyn. Now she is laughing at the Feast, drinking a toast to us all and getting down with her heavenly hosts.

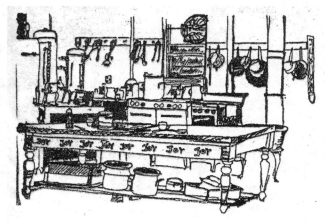

The Kitchen at St. Joseph House, 36 East 1st Street
Artist: Louise Giovannoni

Roland D'Arcangelo (1943–2008)

BY CARMEN TROTTA

The Catholic Worker August–September 2008

OUR DEAR FRIEND ROLAND D'Arcangelo has passed, without word or warning, overnight. Those in the nearest beds heard nothing.

We knew Roland had diabetes and a bad heart, not to mention a two-pack-a-day cigarette habit. Still, the fact is difficult to register. Days later, someone remarked that Roland had been with us for ten years! I had been at the house nearly twenty years and I could not recall a time before Roland. Confounded, I began in earnest to accommodate the facts. In the process I began to recognize the enormity of our loss.

Simply but somewhat abstractly, Roland provided our chaotic house, fraught with the apparent futility of our labors, the surfeit of affection it demands in order to function. The process was entirely unconscious, for him and for us. Natural. Mysterious. A hidden grace. He had no enemies.

He enjoyed everyone, and he was enjoyed by everyone. Now all of those daily interactions are gone. Having taken them largely for granted, we might open ourselves to the salutary ache of missing them. "Blessed," says the Scripture, "are those who mourn."

Roland was a thin-limbed man, with a small head and a large, taut potbelly. Those thin limbs had a stiff, mechanical quality about them. He gestured widely and awkwardly. He stood ramrod straight; or indeed, he seemed often to be arching backwards—this perhaps to displace the weight of his belly. Close-set, lively eyes played above a genuinely beautiful, utterly toothless smile, which was on display pretty regularly. On a good day his hair was a plume of pure white—on others an ungainly, improbable mass—the subject of some teasing mornings on the third floor. Thus, he cut an odd, if not striking, figure.

His clothing only accentuated matters, all from our clothing room, chosen for him by concerned others in the community. If he dressed himself, mismatched socks and clashing colors were par for the course. Ideally, the garments fit "reasonably" well and were "reasonably" clean. Often for convenience's sake, he wore a pullover shirt tucked in below the breast line! It looked absurd, a fact to which he was blissfully oblivious. If you told him he appeared ridiculous, he might acknowledge your comment with a prideful smile, as though he were happy to have momentarily entertained you.

Any portrait of Roland would have to include a cigarette in his hand or mouth. He was a chain smoker, one of those the tips of whose middle and index fingers are stained from orange to brown. He smoked anything, too—menthols, straights, off-brands, typically with a cup of hot coffee and a splash of . . . "No milk, Ro!" (He would have to be warned—milk didn't agree with him.) Most of his disability check went to this habit. We doled out his money to him, otherwise he'd likely have doled it out to others (incapable as he was of not sharing with even the merest acquaintance whatever he possessed), in which case he'd be out of smokes and money well before the end of the month. As it was, we gave him a pack of cigarettes twice each day and five dollars to spend as he chose, and this rarely lasted till midnight.

Thus, in the morning, whoever opened up the kitchen would often have Ro shadowing him, "like white on rice," until the first installment was made. No exchange of niceties, like a "good morning" greeting. He would just walk, literally, two steps behind you, unnerving as a cat between your feet. You might ask for a moment's reprieve, and he would abide, hands folded in front of his belly, staring meekly at you.

We are all, of course, unique, but Roland was unique in an almost provocative way. For most of us, our social selves are highly edited versions of our actual personalities. This was far less true of Roland. He was less egotistical, less guarded, more openly displayed. This was not the result of a refined spirituality. It was more likely the aftermath of trauma and triage. Getting to know Roland was something like inspecting, and coming to admire, the exposed, jerry-rigged plumbing of a squatter's apartment: functional, brilliantly quirky, and without reference to code.

Surely, Roland exhibited many of the signs of a deeply rooted anxiety. He was typically a bit hyperactive and periodically, perhaps cyclically, quite kinetic. Regularly he would venture out on long walks, say from our "East Village" home to Central Park and back—at the very least, 122 blocks. Often he would pace absentmindedly in the kitchen or our tiny backyard or simply sit in a chair rocking his upper body, rhythmically, forward and back.

Related to this, I think, is that each day, for some period of time, Ro would be absorbed into a very solitary, at times motionless, state. That he was inhabiting an otherwise public space made no difference. His consciousness would withdraw from it. At times, he would be expressionless, void, as if in a state of suspended animation. More often, his eyes would fix rigidly on a point just a few inches forward, his face attentive and serious, as though urgently reviewing information rapidly, combating an emergency. Was it a future peril foreseen, or an enormously sad past reviewed? Was it fantasy or a battle to preserve his sanity? Often, merely speaking to him would break the spell. He would "pop out of it" and, quick, like a mime, award you a broad smile, happy to be back among friends. There were other times when he would ward off any disturbance and quickly return to his parallel universe, dark necessity summoning. He might even seek privacy to evade your meddling. It is fearful how little we really know our friends, and how essential the warmth of friendship is to any individual's equilibrium and agency.

We do know of Roland that he was ostracized by his family. He agreed, warily, to help locate them for us, but warned that contacting them was probably not a good idea. I telephoned, and was told in baffling succession that there was no one in the family by that name; that he had died; and, finally, that as far as they were concerned, he was dead. It was a stunning rebuke, at the moment. But, in retrospect, not entirely unimaginable. Remember, Roland was unique in a provocative way, and we knew him only when he was past his prime.

Roland would regularly violate the standard rules of etiquette. For instance, he would never think to comb his hair or bathe unless told to. He was oblivious to matters of appearance, attire, or personal hygiene. He had to be coaxed, cajoled—at times coerced—and assisted with all of that. He would abide by the counsel of friends. But it made little immediate sense to him. Often enough, he would enter the kitchen in the morning, nonchalant, looking for a cup of coffee, rank with the smell of his own urine, a large wet stain on his bedclothes. On each occasion, he would be freshly surprised and disappointed that people had cared to notice. And taken offense! He would comply, reluctantly, with what occurred to him as a time-consuming inconvenience.

Thank heaven Roland was not left to my care alone. Luckily, in the past few years Charles and Brad, Ro's dorm mates, became his default caretakers. Keeping him in clean laundry and insisting he bathe occasionally were the least of their tasks. They became increasingly adept and graceful at what they did—they formed a little community. I misspoke when I said that Roland was "oblivious" to matters of personal hygiene. Although he would never think to initiate the process, certainly, he was physically more comfortable once he was clean. And beyond any thought of causality, there was a joy that accompanied being both clean and cared for that was multiplied and shared in a thousand ways, buoying the life of the larger community.

Roland had no responsibilities, no schedule. If he had been given one, he would have been incapable of adhering to it. Roland slept when he was tired and rose when he woke. Understand, he was literally incapable of *almost* any work. You would have to see it to believe it, but . . . ask him to wipe down a table with a sponge or sweep the floor. He would try, but he could not do it. You could insist and get angry and he would fumble about, enduring your wrath silently, eyes cast downward, cheeks hot with shame. But he could not properly wipe down the table! Or the mattress!

Obviously, this is the voice of experience speaking. And of remorse. My own failures I'll not dwell upon. I, too, get by with a little help from my friends. And Roland absolutely loved me! In fact, I was his favorite. After all, it was I who first invited him to live at St. Joe's. And undoubtedly that was the best thing that ever happened to him. He certainly believed so, and said it. Often.

He came to us a pitiful and haunted figure. It was a bitter winter season, the two radiators near the front door hissing and spitting. On several occasions he just presented himself at the soup line. Filthy, as though he slept on asphalt, he just stepped inside the door, wordless. He seemed to be mute. Frightened, confused, ashamed, he would warily catch your eye and then immediately stare away from you, as though waiting to be noticed and expelled. Sometimes he was still, at other times he could not control himself, and moved about frenetically in the tight space of the foyer, rigidly, like a malfunctioning robot. He was always underdressed. Never a coat or sweater or pair of socks. He never asked for clothes and was uninterested in the offer. What he wanted was food.

Then, one bitterly cold afternoon he presented himself again. This time the cold had seized him. His teeth were chattering and he was barefoot. A heavily soiled pair of boxer shorts and a white undershirt were all he had on. Diarrhea covered the inner thigh of his right leg. Clearly, "the least of these our brethren" had appeared. It would have been criminal not to have received him. Jeremy Scahill and I put him in the shower only to find that he was incapable of bathing himself. We would have to scrub him down—after scraping him down. Afterward we would have to bleach the whole bathroom.

These inauspicious beginnings would proceed for a week while we tried to figure out what to do. We deigned to have our feral Christ figure sleep on the kitchen floor for a time, while we deliberated, faith and fear in rigorous negotiations. As it evolved, the incontinence was persistent. On several mornings we had to clean him—and the kitchen floor. Ever sensible, Joanne Kennedy asked me to take him to Bellevue Hospital to see if they would admit him. He was, of course, immediately admitted. Then, a windfall. Roland had a "prior record," a diagnosis—schizophrenia—a psychotropic cocktail, and a disability check pending. In a couple of weeks the incontinence was largely in check, and thus we received a phone call. As he was not a danger to himself or anyone else, he would not be made a ward of the state. Would we have him back?

"Well . . . yes," and as winter turned to spring Roland came home! In the ensuing thaw certain first impressions melted away. Roland was hardly a mute. He could enjoy a game of spades with Whiskers, Kenneth Terry, and Erich Probst, and he seemed to thrive at the card table banter. Before you knew it, he'd become part of the furniture.

Slowly, he became more assertive and more aspects of his personality emerged. Not long ago, lamenting the current political leadership, Roland informed Jim Reagan that he intended to become the next President and that he wanted Jim to be his VP. He then appointed the late Nat Pace to be Secretary of the Treasury. (Nat was a resident of St. Joe's who always wore a couple of dollars safety-pinned to the breast pocket of his shirt. He was also notorious for losing his money and insisting on his constitutional right to be reimbursed.) He then remarked that he wanted Eugene Solt to be the Speaker of the House. (Again, his wit was on sharp display. Eugene likewise lives in the house and is capable of speaking indefinitely to anyone at any time.)

Occasionally, he would astound the college-educated with a detailed knowledge of some random bit of Americana—like, "Who stabbed Secretary of State Seward the night Lincoln was assassinated?"—or something. This occurred often enough that Tanya and Paul were not afraid to consult with him on the Friday *New York Times* crossword puzzle.

It is ironic that, at his funeral Mass, Joanne Mallesch remembered Roland as a "great greeter." It was true. The mute who could not make eye contact became well known for throwing open his arms and calling out the names of friends entering the house, making them feel as at home as he did. Ideally, for Roland, those open arms would lead to an embrace. That is what he craved most all all. He was no good at this, either! I imagine because he came to it only late in life. His stiff arms would clasp you like a robot, and he would, almost formally, lower his forehead on to your shoulder, and remain there, stiff and immobile. If he could, he would stay there indefinitely. You would always have to tell him to let go. *Deo Gratias.*

Blanche Sargent (1905–2009)

BY FELTON DAVIS

The Catholic Worker October–November 2009

ON MAY 29 WE lost the oldest original resident of Maryhouse, Blanche Louise Sargent from North Carolina, who died of respiratory failure at Mount Sinai Hospital in Queens. Blanche lived down the hall from Miss Day on the second floor in the late 1970s, continued in various rooms (including the notorious "snake room") through the 1980s, and transferred to Coler-Goldwater Hospital on Roosevelt Island in 1990 when Maryhouse simply became too much for her.

It was Blanche who gave me the tour when I arrived and showed me where the plates, bowls, cups, and silverware were kept, and it was Blanche who showed me the barrel where we keep all the used towels, and asked Margaret Murphy if I could have a key to the laundry room so I could make sure the towels were all washed and dried before the next day. After the closet off the dining room, Blanche showed me the "secret stairs" that led up to the library, for when she and Dottie Whaley needed to make a quick getaway following either a food fight in the dining room, or a clothing room riot, which took place often in those years.

Dottie had her job in the auditorium working on the newspaper, and Blanche had her job, which was to go to Sloan's and procure the ice cream for the summertime ice cream parties in the late afternoon. Blanche was the natural pick to go for the ice cream, because she did not require any money. She would just drop a couple quarts of vanilla-chocolate-strawberry into her large bag, and trudge out the door with her walker, and no one would pay her any mind. After Blanche moved out, volunteers would have to actually pay for the ice cream, and the conscientious ones would get awful, tasteless, sugar-free ice cream.

Blanche's instructions to new volunteers were not delivered with nearly the volume of Sister Jeanette's thunderous commands, but she did get her two cents' worth in. As far as the silverware was concerned, Blanche explained that workers were not rinsing the knives, forks, and spoons sufficiently, and that the rinse water was quickly becoming so soapy as to be useless. As far as the lint screen in the dryer was concerned, her firm conviction was that a thick wad of lint meant that people from St. Joseph House had been allowed to use the machines. As far as the second floor television room was concerned, Blanche wanted me to understand clearly that Mary and Helgi were in charge of selecting what programs were viewed.

Blanche was one who never used the word "crabby" in connection with Miss Day. Frank has letters that Dorothy Day received from Blanche, handwritten notes of gratitude for a warm coat, or some other consideration that had been accorded her, and when I arrived in 1988, Blanche was still claiming that Miss Day had not died, so it was premature for us to mourn.

When she was ready to make her own departure, she stripped down to nothing and stood in the chapel with her arms outstretched toward the altar, as if to say, "Naked I came into the world, and naked I will return." She was ready, but her Maker had other ideas. Blanche was clearly one of the most well liked, and continued as Maryhouse royalty long after she transferred to Coler-Goldwater Hospital. Sister Jeanette, in particular, told me never to visit Blanche without first consulting her, whereupon she would rearrange her busy schedule in order to go with me, or at least take up a collection to buy some snacks for Blanche. First, she would go to Annie Skwarek and beg a couple of bucks, then she would go to Gloria, who would kick in most generously, and Sister Jeanette would make up the rest from her own funds.

A care package for Blanche began with a couple of pieces of fried chicken, a dollar bag of barbecued potato chips, possibly a grilled cheese and tomato sandwich, and then, when we got to the nursing home, Sister Jeanette would want to stop in the cafeteria for coffee to wash all this down. Sister Jeanette was diabetic and wasn't supposed to have any sugar in her coffee, but on Roosevelt Island we were well out of range of the sugar police. Anyway, we knew that Blanche liked nearly unlimited sugar in her coffee, so it wouldn't be appropriate for us to take ours black while Blanche was emptying five or six packets of sugar into hers.

And then we arrived one day and found the bed empty. My heart skipped a beat when I considered the implications, but Sister Jeanette was already on her way to the nurses' station to demand an explanation. Blanche had been temporarily moved to Metropolitan Hospital across the river with a bad case of pneumonia, and Sister Jeanette immediately commanded me to make the arrangements for us to go there, even if it required cab fare. She would pay for it, because we absolutely had to see Blanche one last time. (This "one last time" was in 1991, maybe.) Sister Jeanette wasn't going to spend the rest of her life full of regret for having abandoned Blanche in her final hour, so off we went. We found Blanche with an oxygen mask over her nose, and an IV of antibiotics in her arm. She seemed just barely to be breathing, and for Sister Jeanette that was enough. She looked around and then said perfunctorily, "There's no priest here. You understand me? They got no priest here to do the right thing."

Added to my numerous other failings in Sister Jeanette's sight was that I didn't carry around with me one of those prayer books with the ceremony of the Last Rites in it, nor did I have the necessary words memorized. None of that cut it with Sister Jeanette, who said very sharply, "Get over there!" motioning me to the other side of the bed. "We have to do the right thing, that's all there is to it. Take Blanche's hand." I did as I was instructed, and then Sister Jeanette put her hand over mine, leaned in close to the unresponsive Blanche, and delivered some of the most moving words of comfort and consolation I have ever heard.

"Blanche Sargent, you're not alone here. You don't have to go—I mean you don't have to go alone, all by yourself. It's me, it's Jeanette, and you know—what's his name. We're with you here in the hospital. We haven't forgotten you, not even for one day. You understand me? Now let me explain what's happening now. Upstairs—where you're going—you're gonna meet up with—okay, probably everybody you ever knew. They're all gonna be there. Your family, your parents, and Annie Skwarek, and Anna who lived up on the fourth floor, old Hungarian Anna, and Helgi, and Lena, and Lucy, and Miss Day. Miss Day will be there, I'm sure of that. Darphy found a room for you in this world, and she's got a room for you in the next. You understand what I'm saying, Blanche? Darphy's gotta place for you, and that's where you're going now. Okay? Now we're going to say the words, the right words. We're going to do the right thing for you here, because they got no priest."

Sister Jeanette's version of the ceremony of the Last Rites went very smoothly—somewhat improvisational but full of earnest entreaties to all concerned powers that be in the next world to make sure everything was properly arranged for the new arrival. It ended with the twenty-third Psalm. Then we let go of Blanche's hand and Sister Jeanette motioned me out of the room quickly, saying, "Okay, let's get the hell out of here."

Sister Jeanette kept making the trip until her legs became too weak, but was followed by a long series of replacement visitors, none so faithful as Blanche's mainstay, Kassie Temple. Kassie knew where to find the perfect undies for Blanche, and also the perfect handkerchief, and had impeccable choices when it came to reading matter (*Cosmopolitan*, *Vogue*, *People*, or *Redbook*, rather than the latest issue of *The Catholic Worker*).

As long as Kassie was on the horizon, Blanche stayed awake and interested in what was going on at Maryhouse, and so it was particularly painful to find that when Kassie died in 2002, we could neither explain to Blanche what happened, nor make up for the lack of care and individual attention. Blanche just kept on asking for Kassie, for months on end, and finally gave up and stopped speaking to any of us in the spring of 2003. Robert made up a basket of flowers for her on Easter in 2004, and she took hold of the basket and said the word, "Beautiful." That was the last word any of us heard from her.

Blanche was 103 when all life support was removed, and her strong and stubborn heart continued to beat for hours. Thank you to Father Josephian of Our Lady of Mount Carmel for administering the Last Rites a second time, and thanks especially to the nurses on the second floor of Mount Sinai, who attended Blanche's final hours and made every effort to keep her comfortable. Her wake was held at Ortiz Funeral Home, and had to take place in the larger room because there were too many ghosts of Maryhouse past to fit into the smaller chapel. Matt Tessitore and I accompanied the casket out to Rosemount Cemetery in Elizabeth, New Jersey.

In the days following Blanche's departure, many friends and former Maryhouse volunteers sent condolences and memories. One of the most moving was from Elaine Ess, now living in Minnesota:

"What word comes to mind when I think of Blanche is her graciousness. She had the sweet southern voice inquiring politely about my family, other things going on at the house, or the other ladies at Maryhouse. She had patience with the new workers, like me, who inadvertently made mistakes regarding the unwritten rules of the house. She would overlook the offense and tactfully move onto the next subject. At times, she would get annoyed about things and then fire off in a voice that revealed an inner spirit and steely strength that always caught me by surprise. Fortunately, the next day, all was back to the kind, gracious, and sweet lady we all knew. Graciousness is an underrated value today. The ability to be genuinely interested in others, overlooking offenses, being courteous and showing kindness. I'm glad Blanche taught me those lessons by example."

New York City Street Scene
Artist: Rita Corbin

Joseph P. Foth (1945–2009)

BY JOE MCKENZIE-HAMILTON

The Catholic Worker December 2009

FOR ALL THE YEARS I've been in and around the New York City Catholic Worker, there have been certain enduring fixtures—both people and things that seem like they have always been there, and surely, I think, will always be there. These elements are ingrained in my sense of the community, and for me make up essential parts of the landscape, shape, and spirit of St. Joe's. I think of the stone statue of St. Joseph that sits in the window, rubbed shiny in spots where decades of tired hands in tactile prayer have laid their burdens and hopes. I think too of the large, thick wood and steel table that dominates the kitchen. How many meals have been prepared here, day in and day out? How many times have we gathered here for the breaking of the bread and the sharing of the cup, in seasons gentle and seasons jarring? And now, in this season of our mourning, I think especially of our recently departed Joe Foth, who seemed always to have been here, always a necessary part of the house, always a noticeable presence in the community.

Joe was quite a figure, distinct in many ways. He stood out for his height; indeed, he was our Big Joe, to distinguish him from all our other Joes, myself included. We had a Little Joe as well, so I jokingly wondered with Joe in my early days what my nickname should be. "How about Funny Looking Joe?" he responded without missing a beat. Though accurate enough, I'm glad it never stuck.

Joe had his usual outfit of a T-shirt or plaid shirt, jeans, and work boots, usually with a hand-rolled cigarette in his mouth. But perhaps what stood out most clearly was his voice, loud and clear, and laced with a very strong Brooklyn accent straight out of *The Honeymooners*. That voice was coupled with his weary, knowing laugh at our ignorance of all the things only he knew. That voice that carried such a quick wit was also our window into his strengths and struggles.

That voice showed his humor. Seeing us sitting around the kitchen during a rare slow moment on a house shift, Joe would walk by muttering about all of the "chair magnets" in this place. He also liked word play, proclaiming under his breath that he was "fobody's nool!" Having a great fondness for jokes, he had a repertoire that he would regularly expand, revise, and edit. "A priest, a minister, and a rabbi walk into a bar, and the bartender says, 'What is this—a joke?'" Joe would deliver it almost always with his trademark, crooked smile.

I also recall a time when a lovely oil painting of St. Francis embracing Lady Poverty, created by our late, beloved Tony Gawron, went missing from the wall. A thorough search ensued, and though a bevy of always needed and frequently missing spoons and coffee cups was discovered, the painting was not, until an alert person noticed something odd about Joe's mattress. We checked, and hidden there was St. Francis. Joe, with some smiling chagrin, said he needed a board to keep the mattress firm. Somehow, I think both St. Francis and Lady Poverty would have been delighted to have been in service to Big Joe.

That voice showed his hardship, too. His comments and conversations illuminated the underlying paranoia and delusional thinking of a serious and persistent mental illness. Joe referenced the thieves and murderers who lurked about. He'd laugh ruefully at their insidiousness, and how naive we were not to know about all they were up to. Joe was convinced they put cat urine in the soup, and occasionally would helpfully share this while walking through the morning soup line. After such a remark, a few people would add an extra dose of our homemade (very) hot sauce, rumored to be strong enough to burn through anything, just to be on the safe side. Joe's worries were real to him, and once drove him to sneak our two house cats out to the Marble Cemetery on Second Street. Regrettably, only one was found and returned home.

The mental illness Joe lived with was relentless. Medications helped mitigate and manage the cruel symptoms, but could not cure the illness. Sometimes it was too much for Joe and he would self-medicate with alcohol to relieve the torment. It was tough to see him in such a state. In my earlier days here, I remember the alcohol occasionally making him loud, even aggressive. We would ask him to stay outside until he sobered up, but he wasn't always agreeable, and would knock loudly at our door. He was a survivor, smart and resourceful. I recall one such occasion when he was kept out and would have none of it. A few minutes after he was hound-dogging on the front stoop, a swarm of police officers were at the door responding to an urgent 911 call about a violent disturbance on the second floor, Joe's home of many years. The clutter of cops crowded in, himself in the middle of them, trying to look inconspicuous, nonchalantly heading towards the stairs. Though the ruse didn't work, we had to admire his ingenuity. After such a night, Joe was usually very remorseful the next day, and was unusually solicitous and helpful around the kitchen. He promised to be "strictly AA" from there on in, and we wished serenity for him.

Joe was a man of faith, not a soft and fuzzy kind, but rather a faith hard won, of someone who knew deeply the terrible beauty of the world. He would sometimes come to our evening Vespers in the kitchen. I have fond memories of our beloved Bishop of blessed memory, Arthur J. Lacey, struggling to be patient as Joe prayed the Our Father rapidly in his strong Brooklyn tones and Nat Pace, also of blessed memory and Joe's long time floormate, would enunciate and caress each syllable in a slow, melodious style. Yet perhaps the most striking, poignant prayers Joe made were that he be relieved of his mental sufferings. This was a prayer from the depths of his being, from the heart of a painful, lifelong struggle. Only in death has he finally found the fullness of peace.

We give thanks for this big man who lived for year upon countless year here. I am eternally grateful that he found a home at St. Joe's. He found connection and community in this welcoming place. In this season of Advent, this time of anticipation and hope, in our daily work, at once hard and hopeful, we look for a time when all those who are considered least and left out find a home where we can all live fully and freely, alive in the love of God and one another.

Charles Payne (1942–2011)

BY SILKE TUDOR

The Catholic Worker January–February 2012

> Do not gentle into that good night,
> Old age should burn and rave at close of day;
> Rage, rage against the dying of the light.

DYLAN THOMAS

CHARLIE SOMETIMES SPOKE OF the great love of his life. She was a gorgeous woman, a class act by all accounts. "Oh yeah, she could charm the birds out of the trees," he'd say with a conspiratorial wink. "We tried to kill each other on more than one occasion."

The occasion he spoke of the most kicked off one summer day down at the track. The exact events shifted according to his mood, but the cause was always the same. "We drank like fish. Some nights she could out-drink me." Charlie's snow-white eyebrows would rise to illustrate the enormity of the latter statement. "She did anything, ups, downs, it didn't matter. But I liked speed. Bennies, Black Beauties, Mollies . . ."

It wasn't hard to imagine Charlie on speed. When Charlie first came to the Worker, it wasn't through the typical channel of group consensus, but through the back door as a friend of Roger O'Neil. (Ever the exception, Charlie would have hated the idea of coming in like everyone else, anyway.) On Saturday mornings, which was Roger's shift for years, Charlie became a force in the kitchen, lording over the ten-burner stove, wielding a huge spatula like a weapon, and taking orders for eggs which were an expectation, not a prerogative. If you were lucky, the breakfast orders came in at a slow steady pace. If you were not so lucky, there was a lull in the action, and Charlie would sweep through the dining room, grabbing every cup and plate in sight, tossing them into the sink at a breakneck pace (sometimes they did break). It didn't matter whether you were finished or not. If you dared protest, Charlie would holler invectives or slam the plate down in disgust before he whirled off again. He had to keep moving. Long after he got sober, Charlie could not sit still. Ever.

Charlie's kinetic nature had its advantages. He was the natural house-keeper on the third floor, which he came to call home. He scrubbed the bathroom, mopped the floor, and then sprayed the air with can after can of air freshener. ("Keeps the bugs away," he'd say.) When Roland was still alive, Charlie would berate him into washing, which wasn't such a bad thing. After Roland died, Charlie was ever arranging and rearranging the small coffee nook he built up in his place with found furniture. Charlie's taste was somewhat questionable, running the gamut from giant plastic peanuts and neon beer signs to broken *shoji* screens and larger-than-life portraits of Bill Wilson, but the fellas liked the nook. It was a place to socialize away from the hustle and bustle of the kitchen. And there were always plenty of sweets, often tucked away in drawers or under the bed (which did little to keep away the bugs).

Charlie's sweet tooth was notorious. On the Sunday nights when the donation truck arrived, folks would be in the basement sorting produce while Charlie was in the kitchen ferreting away garbage bags full of donuts. It used to drive Jim crazy. But the sweets weren't all for Charlie. By the time Charlie came to the Catholic Worker, he was dedicated to AA. Every morn-ing before five he would trundle off to help set up coffee (and presumably the donuts) at the meeting where he got clean. Supplying sugar for all.

"Some of those guys only come for the sweets," explained Charlie. "Real low bottom cases. It's important I be there for them."

In AA, they knew Charlie as Lucky, as did a lot of old-timers on the street. Back in the day, Lucky hustled money in a top coat and tails which he stored in the heating vent of a bathroom in a fancy hotel in midtown.

"I made sure I looked nice," he said. It wasn't hard to imagine. Char-lie's beard was always clipped with precision, his thick white hair perfectly combed. "And I knew how to talk to those people. I could maitre d' at any of those fancy hotels."

To hear Charlie tell it, and there was no reason to doubt it, he was once in the entertainment business, managing some hot jazz club for a bookie downtown.

"I could drink anywhere in town for free. I got written up in the newspaper. I was a real bigshot," said Charlie. "I even threw a big benefit show for the homeless . . . but I pocketed the money."

Eventually, drugs and alcohol got the best of him. And, somewhere during that downward slide, Charlie met his love. "She hustled the fancy hotels, too. One day she told me to meet her at this upscale restaurant with a bar. As I walked in she was being escorted out by two cops . . . I never saw her again." Why? "I didn't know her real name. She always lied . . . She lied, I lied . . . Such a beautiful fiction."

Charlie sang one song, a gorgeous Spanish love ballad that earned him spare change. That song could break your heart. After Charlie got sick, he sang it to me a lot. No one knows exactly what happened. One day Charlie walked out the front door of St. Joe's, and didn't come back for several months. He never called, but when he showed up again he'd had an emergency colostomy operation. His balance was bad. His memory was bad. He looked like a skeleton. He had come home to to die. But he didn't die.

Charlie had always been a very proud, very private man. By the time we really needed to know things about him, details were vague in his mind. He had a sister, maybe a brother. Maybe in Boston. His mother was born in Nova Scotia, a stunning woman, a strong woman (the tales of abuse dissolved with his memory). The Social Security number he provided was most likely the building block of one of those beautiful fictions. It didn't match anything. But somehow, by some miracle (Joanne had made a novena when I was trying to get him Medicare), a social worker took pity on us and gave him health insurance. And we learned to take care of Charlie as best we could. It wasn't easy. He didn't want us to. It was messy, and Charlie was prone to rages which worsened along with his memory. Losing himself made him afraid. He often begged doctors to let him die. But he held on.

Sometimes his memory worked in mysterious ways. He talked a lot about AA, about folks he had met once or twice who hadn't made it, about the people from the Catholic Worker, those who had passed away before him, those who had cared for him, and always Roger O'Neil.

Once he grabbed my arm and squeezed it hard, searching my face intently. "St. Joseph House is the only real home I've ever had." He often spoke of God. And sometimes, when he was feeling pretty good, his mind drifted towards a woman, and a long beautiful fiction.

Acknowledgments

We are grateful for those whose lives we glimpse in these pages,

For those who paid attention, remembered, and wrote,

For those who read, prayed, and worked with us on this journey.

We are grateful also for Meg Hyre, whose careful work and thoughtful mind helped this project come to fruition.

Thank you.

Addendum

AT THE TIME OF this writing, the Catholic Worker movement is made up of over two hundred communities, houses, farms, and collectives around the world. Each one has its own name, its own special work, and its own way of responding in faith to the issues of poverty, war, and violence at every level of our society.

To subscribe to *The Catholic Worker* newspaper, please contact the New York Catholic Worker at Maryhouse, 55 East 3rd Street, New York, NY 10003. (212) 777-9617.

For more information on the history of the Catholic Worker, a full bibliography, and a list of communities, please visit www.catholicworker. org.